THE NATIONAL INSTITUTE OF
ECONOMIC AND SOCIAL RESEARCH

Occasional Papers
XLIII

YOUTH UNEMPLOYMENT IN GREAT BRITAIN

YOUTH UNEMPLOYMENT IN GREAT BRITAIN

P. E. HART

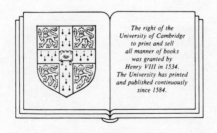

The right of the
University of Cambridge
to print and sell
all manner of books
was granted by
Henry VIII in 1534.
The University has printed
and published continuously
since 1584.

CAMBRIDGE UNIVERSITY PRESS

CAMBRIDGE

NEW YORK   NEW ROCHELLE   MELBOURNE   SYDNEY

Published by the Press Syndicate of the University of Cambridge
The Pitt Building, Trumpington Street, Cambridge CB2 1RP
32 East 57th Street, New York, NY 10022, USA
10 Stamford Road, Oakleigh, Melbourne 3166, Australia

First published 1988

Printed in Great Britain at The Bath Press, Avon

British Library cataloguing in publication data
Hart, P. E.
Youth unemployment in Great Britain.
1. Youth – Employment – Great Britain
2. Unemployment – Great Britain
I. Title
331.3'4137941   HD6276.G7

Library of Congress cataloguing in publication data
Hart, P. E. (Peter Edward)
Youth unemployment in Great Britain.
(The National Institute of Economic and Social
Research occasional papers; 43)
1. Youth – Employment – Great Britain. 2. Unemployment
– Great Britain. I. Title. II. Series: Occasional
papers (National Institute of Economic and Social
Research(; 43.
HD6276.G72H37   1988   331.3'4137941   87-25597

ISBN 0 521 35348 3

CONTENTS

TABLES

SYMBOLS IN THE TABLES
... not available
— nil or negligible
n.a. not applicable

CHARTS

PREFACE

This book is concerned with the long-term upward trend in youth unemployment, rather than with its short-term fluctuations through the trade cycle. Why has the rate of youth unemployment tended to become higher with each successive economic recession? How can this upward trend be reversed? These important questions involve many complex issues which are usually summarised by an economic model. Answers are derived from the model in the belief that its properties approximate those of the economy. But different schools of thought use different models and, as we shall see, the available statistical data are insufficient to enable us to make a rational choice between them based on rigorous econometric tests. Meanwhile high youth unemployment persists.

Instead of attempting to discriminate between different economic theories, this study aims to formulate, and justify, policies to reduce youth unemployment which are likely to be acceptable to the different schools of thought. Even this strictly pragmatic approach sometimes involves complicated technical matters, but as far as possible they are consigned to notes and appendices.

I am extremely grateful to Andrew Britton, the Director of the National Institute of Economic and Social Research, for inviting me to undertake this study and for his most helpful criticism of earlier drafts. I have also benefited from the comments of Andres Drobny, John Ermisch, Brian Henry, Kit Jones, Sig Prais, Chris Trinder, Karin Wagner and David Worswick of the NIESR, David Marsden of the LSE, and Mark Casson, Paul Cheshire, Geoffrey Maynard, Kerry Patterson, Jim Pemberton and Neville Waites of the University of Reading. It is a pleasure to thank them for their generous help, while at the same time absolving them from responsibility for any of the conclusions reached here. I am also indebted to an anonymous referee for comments which led to the addition of Chapter 8 on the spatial aspects of youth unemployment.

Finally, I should like to thank Mrs J. Dare, Mrs D. Swan and Mrs P. Watts for computing assistance, Mrs A. Wright for typing the book and Mrs F. Robinson for preparing it for the press.

National Institute of Economic   P. E. HART
and Social Research
London, August 1987

THE RISE OF YOUTH UNEMPLOYMENT

INTRODUCTION

Between 1951 and 1981 unemployment rates for young people under eighteen years increased from 1 per cent to about 25 per cent. Without the Youth Training Scheme and Special Employment measures, the current youth unemployment rate might well be nearer 50 per cent.[1] The basic time series on youth unemployment to 1981 are surveyed in Chapter 2, which also summarises the more recent but non-comparable data since then. If the young are defined as those under 25 years old, to facilitate comparisons with France and Germany, the youth unemployment rate reached 21.5 per cent in 1985. Of course, young people might have higher unemployment rates than adults because it takes time to find the most suitable job, and unemployment spells arise as youngsters search for an optimum. But over 600,000 young people under 25 years have been out of work for over six months and the job search explanation hardly seems appropriate. Why has youth unemployment in the United Kingdom risen to unprecedented levels? Even in 1931 the unemployment rates were less than 12 per cent for males, and less than 8 per cent for females under twenty years, as shown in table 2.5.

Youth unemployment is such a large part of aggregate unemployment and the two are so highly correlated, as shown in Chapter 2, that any satisfactory explanation of its dramatic rise must refer to standard economic theories of aggregate unemployment, such as those of the neo-classical, Keynesian and structuralist schools of thought;[2] that is, whatever creates adult unemployment is highly likely to create youth unemployment. But because the upward trend of youth unemployment was even greater than that of adult unemployment, additional forces are likely to have had a special effect on the employment of young people. For example, any satisfactory explanation of the rise of youth unemployment must also include the long-term forces of demographic and technological change. The number of young people aged 15–19 years increased between 1970 and 1982, exacerbating the problem of rising youth unemployment, and then began to decline. The number of 20–24 year olds has been increasing since 1975 and begins to decrease in 1987, thus unemployment for this age group will also be eased by demographic changes. These effects are discussed in Chapter 4 on the supply of young labour.

The important structural changes include the increasing use of sophisticated machinery requiring the use of skilled labour especially in manufacturing, and the increasing employment of married women part-time workers instead of full-time workers, especially in the financial, service and distributive trades. The theory of the firm pays most attention to industry and naturally leads to greater emphasis being placed on technological change and automation as causes of unemployment. Yet manufacturing now employs less than 26 per cent of the total labour force, compared with nearly 60 per cent employed in finance, distribution and services. More attention should be paid to employment in the non-manufacturing trades, particularly to the distributive trades discussed in Chapter 7 which have traditionally been a major source of jobs for youngsters. In any event, both types of change in manufacturing and non-manufacturing have reduced the scope for the employment of unskilled youngsters who need full-time jobs. Moreover, the effects of both on the labour market have been accentuated by the tax system in the United Kingdom, as shown later in the section on structural explanations of unemployment. But let us first consider the neo-classical and Keynesian approaches to the explanation of the rise in youth unemployment.

THE NEO-CLASSICAL APPROACH

Neo-classical economists claim that the supply and demand for young workers are brought into equilibrium by changes in their wage rates relative to prices of other inputs. The labour market is like the market for commodities. If it does not appear to produce an equilibrium, some institutional impediment must be hindering the natural tendency for markets to be self-equilibrating. Possible impediments include the excessively high relative wages of young people fixed by trade union bargaining, the lack of geographical mobility produced by government intervention in the housing market, the voluntary unemployment produced by unemployment and social security benefits, and the reluctance of employers to recruit young labour following the various employment protection laws which in particular reduce the job chances of new entrants into the labour market. To reverse the upward trend in youth unemployment involves, according to this approach, repealing minimum wage legislation and employment protection laws, abolishing rent control, weakening the power of trade unions, and reducing the real value of benefits. The Government has adopted some of these policies, such as excluding the wages of young people from the minima set by Wages Councils, and relaxing some of the provisions of the employment protection legislation.[3] What is the evidence to justify such policies?

Chapter 3 reviews seven econometric investigations of the effect of the relative wages of young people on their relative employment. At first sight, the claim that high relative wages cause youth unemployment seems impressive; six studies conclude that the high wages of young people relative to adults' wages have reduced their employment. However, closer examination reveals that these econometric results are not firmly established. The six studies use time series of relative wages derived from the Department of Employment's October Inquiry which is unrepresentative of young people's wages because it omits important non-manufacturing sectors such as distribution. The New Earnings Survey is more representative but a seventh study based on these figures finds no significant effect of variations in relative wages on youth unemployment. Unfortunately, even the New Earnings Survey suffers from the major drawback that the earnings of part-time workers below the national insurance threshold, the very workers who are being substituted for young people, are excluded.

But while the most rigorous neo-classical economic models may not help to explain the rise of youth unemployment, the basic emphasis on the importance of the effect of relative wages may well be justified. As shown in Chapter 6, the relative pay of apprentices in Germany is much lower than in the United Kingdom and so German firms, unlike British firms, can afford to train youngsters in the techniques required to operate, maintain and repair the complicated capital equipment used in modern production. The result is that German manufacturers have a competitive advantage over British manufacturers in global markets because of the higher skill content of their products. In terms of the derived demand for young labour, the unskilled, unqualified British nineteen year olds cannot compete in international markets with skilled, qualified German nineteen year olds and hence find it difficult to obtain employment. Thus some young people in the United Kingdom may become unemployed because their high relative wages discourage employers from providing the training necessary for skilled jobs which are available.

The idea that unemployment is largely voluntary, created by over-generous unemployment and social security benefits, is very familiar and is discussed in Chapter 4. There is an immense literature on the subject but it has been found difficult to measure these effects, which in any case are probably very small. Of course, the measurement techniques used reflect average behaviour and are consistent with the serious, but atypical, abuses of the benefit system highlighted by the newspapers.

The effects of employment protection legislation on the recruitment of labour also appear to be small. As shown in Chapter 5 on the demand for labour, three separate surveys of employers have been unable to find any substantial effect of unfair dismissal on the amount of labour hired. Geographical immobility of labour is probably less serious a problem for young people than for adults; unemployed youngsters are in the market for lodgings rather than for houses, and are therefore more mobile than adults. Thus the main factor explaining the rise of youth unemployment drawn from the neo-classical approach appears to be the effect of the relative wages of young people. The high wages of youngsters compared with those of adults have been a disincentive to employers to provide the training for skilled jobs at a time when technological change is reducing the demand for unskilled labour. Moreover, an individual firm has little incentive to provide the expensive training required to provide its own supply of skilled workers, because it justifiably fears that other firms will 'poach' its skilled labour when their apprenticeships are finished. Hence youth unemployment is high and yet a shortage of skilled labour persists.[4] Clearly, externalities are important and the labour market is not self-equilibrating.

THE KEYNESIAN APPROACH

Keynes' General Theory is concerned with the short run rather than the long run and logically a Keynesian approach to explaining the enormous increase in youth unemployment since 1951 would have to emphasise short-term disturbances at the expense of long-term causes. It might be argued, for example, that while youth unemployment rates increased from around 1 per cent in 1951 to near 7 per cent by 1972 the really significant increases followed the sharp rises in oil prices produced by OPEC. The youth unemployment rate increased from around 4 per cent in 1973 to some 20 per cent in 1977, and from about 15 per cent in 1979 to over 25 per cent by 1981 and was even higher by 1982. A Keynesian might claim that the massive short-term increases in unemployment resulted from the deflationary policies pursued by country after country while attempting to adjust for increased oil prices. Any country trying to avoid a restrictionist policy was compelled to follow suit by the resulting pressure on its balance of payments and/or its exchange rate. In the United Kingdom the fall in aggregate demand was particularly marked after 1979. The policies of the Conservative Government, coupled with the high sterling exchange rate associated with the sale of North Sea oil, may have reduced inflation, but they destroyed jobs in manufacturing industry on a massive scale. Markets lost when the sterling exchange rate rose to a peak in 1982 could not be regained when the exchange rate fell to a trough in 1985.

This type of diagnosis regards the rise of youth unemployment simply as part of the rise of general unemployment produced by a deficiency in aggregate demand. However, it has long been recognised that an expansion of demand achieved by increased Government expenditure might lead to increases in prices, wages and imports rather than to increases in domestic output and employment.[5] Questions which arise include the extent to which the rise in unemployment is due to demand deficiency, or to our past failure to control inflation when demand is expanded. Alternatively, the fundamental cause of the upward trend in unemployment may be our lack of international competitiveness, which results in a high marginal propensity to import. These central economic issues are important for the explanation of the rise of unemployment in general, and youth unemployment in particular, and reappear in Chapter 5 and in the section on demand policies in Chapter 9. Meanwhile, let us turn to structural unemployment.

THE STRUCTURALIST APPROACH

Those who emphasise structural explanations of unemployment do not believe that the economy is self-equilibrating and have this in common with Keynesians. But unlike the latter they think that a one-sector model of the economy is inadequate to analyse the economy.[6] At the very least a two-sector model reveals the fundamental causes of youth unemployment which are hidden by Keynesian analysis. Let us disaggregate the economy into two sectors, 1 and 2, and let sector 1 be prosperous and expanding while sector 2 is the opposite. Let us also suppose that money wages are rigid downwards and flexible upwards. (All these assumptions are justified in Appendix 2.) In this model the unemployed in sector 2 cannot obtain jobs in sector 1. In a boom, sector 1 adjusts to the excess demand for its products mainly by increasing wages and prices and does not absorb the unemployed from sector 2. Moreover, the unemployed in sector 2 cannot bid down money wages in sector 1 for many reasons. They may not have the necessary skills and cannot obtain employment in sector 1. Trade union closed shops in sector 1 will not allow them to have union cards. The carefully negotiated wage scales in sector 1 cannot be lowered merely because unemployed young people in sector 2 are prepared to work for less money: after all, any such lowering of a salary scale might reduce the remuneration of those at the top of the scale who take the decisions to recruit! In any case, the prosperous firms in sector 1 may be located far away from the parental homes of the young unemployed in sector 2 and such young people cannot afford to move to the prosperous areas where accommodation (including lodgings) is likely to be much more expensive.

In reality the number of sectors is much greater than two. The two-sector model is simply a theoretical device to illustrate the limitations of a one-sector model. Structural changes are required to reduce structural unemployment. A monetarist policy which relies on the price mechanism will merely increase unemployment in sector 2 without necessarily halting the increase in prices and wages in sector 1. A Keynesian policy of expanding aggregate demand will increase wages and prices, but not output, in sector 1 and its inflationary effects will probably outweigh the benefits of any increase in output and employment in sector 2.

A more detailed discussion of structural unemployment is provided by Standing (1983) who specifies seven causes: (i) changes in industrial structure, (ii) mismatch of skills, (iii) geographical mismatch, (iv) demographic shifts, (v) institutional rigidities, (vi) 'unemployability' and (vii) capital restructuring. His allegation that references to structural unemployment are often vague has some justification. The two-sector model provides a formal statement of the barriers which impede adjustment, but although it may more closely approximate the behaviour of the labour market than the one-sector model, it is still far removed from the segmented labour market in the real world.

The concept of structural unemployment is not new. It featured prominently in the deliberations of the Committee of Economists (Keynes, Henderson, Pigou, Robbins and Stamp) which reported to the Economic Advisory Council (chaired by the Prime Minister, Mr J. R. MacDonald) in 1930. The failure of British industry to adapt quickly enough to changed economic circumstances after the First World War received considerable attention from economists, especially from those writing before the widespread acceptance of Keynes' General Theory, for example, Pigou (1927), Clay (1929), Cannan (1930) and Pool (1938). Furthermore, the makers of economic policy clearly recognised in 1944 that maintaining total expenditure was not sufficient to provide full employment and a whole chapter in the famous White Paper on Employment Policy (*Cmd.* 6527 1944) was devoted to structural problems.

More recently Willke (1982) has emphasised structural unemployment in Germany. Product and labour markets are heterogeneous and hence some disaggregation below the macroeconomic level increases our understanding of the economy. Disequilibrium transactions do take place, contrary to Walrasian theory. Asymmetries are common in economic life; excess supplies induce little or no price or wage reductions and lead to unemployment, whereas excess demands induce appreciable increases in prices and wages and little expansion of employment. Thus we have inflation and unemployment. A more rigorous formal development of structural unemployment in a two-sector theoretical model is provided by Casson (1983). A disaggregation of macroeconomic analysis is not carried out merely to provide more detail; it is an essential part of exposing the sectoral asymmetries which are hidden by aggregation.

In his survey of research into unemployment, Nickell (1982) summarised the statistical difficulties which arise when attempting to measure structural unemployment, using UV (unemployment and vacancies) analysis, and concluded that 'the whole area of structural unemployment is more or less one vast unknown'. Structural unemployment has been defined in an earlier National Institute study by Cheshire (1973) as the minimum of either (a) the total excesses of vacancies over unemployment in all sectors with such an excess, or (b) the total excesses of unemployment over vacancies in all sectors with such an excess. But this standard UV analysis raises many problems.

First, the propensity to register V is less than that for U; in fact only about 30 per cent of vacancies in the United Kingdom are reported in official statistics. Thus any recorded excess of V over U is biased downwards. Furthermore, as emphasised by Willke (1982) and Casson (1983) because of the asymmetrical behaviour of prices and wages, it is possible for unfilled vacancies in the prosperous sector to be removed by the bidding up of wages, with unemployment persisting in the declining sector. Thus the structural mismatch would be reflected not in the high V in the prosperous sector but in the high wages in that sector. In the present context, high youth unemployment, and high adult wages in the prosperous industries, could occur together. Thus the claims of the UV analyst that structural unemployment is less important than the deficiency of aggregate demand might not be justified. In particular, a recent survey of UV measures of structural unemployment by Jackman and Roper (1985), which concluded that industrial restructuring had not had much effect on aggregate unemployment, merely reflects the narrowness of the UV measures of structural unemployment, as explained in Appendix 2.

Of course UV analysis was not in the minds of the Committee of Economists in the 1930s, nor does it feature in the analysis of the economic historians or of industrial economists who study structural unemployment. For them, structural unemployment has a broader interpretation, linked with slowness in the adaptation to economic change. Dogged resistance to change has been attributed by Olson (1982) to collusions and distributional coalitions including the restrictive practices of labour and of firms. The result is an inefficient use of existing resources, a lack of response to new market opportunities, low productivity and low profitability. In turn these have discouraged investment in new processes and skills. The lack of such investment perpetuates structural unemployment ... and so the resistance to change continues. Such fundamental problems are of the utmost importance and may well explain the rise and decline

of nations as Olson (1982) suggests, but they are not captured by the
UV measures of structural unemployment.

CONCLUSION

Three different types of explanation of the rise in youth unemployment
have been summarised. More details of each may be found in Standing
(1983), Morris and Sinclair (1985),[7] Lindbeck and Snower (1985)[8] and
in their references. Each school of thought has sub-divisions within it
because different economists attach different weights to particular parts
of their explanations. Furthermore, some economists regard different
models as closer approximations to reality at different times so that a
model appropriate for the United Kingdom in 1930 is not necessarily
useful in 1970 or 1980. But it is generally understood that the neo-classical, Keynesian, and structuralist theories are only models (or scientific
research programmes) of a very complex real economy. Moreover, this
economy is subjected to major shocks.

Young people entering the labour market now face a world of intense
competition. Their parents, entering the labour market in the 1950s and
1960s, did not have to cope with such severe competition from manufacturing imports from other countries in the European Community, or
from the newly industrialised countries in the Far East. Nor did they
have to worry about multinational enterprises switching output from
their British factories to their overseas plants. Fundamental changes in
industrial structure are taking place. One important change is the growing proportion of part-time workers. To an increasing extent firms are
employing a central core of full-time, skilled and experienced workers
and a penumbra of part-time or casual workers who are usually
unskilled.[9] Young people need full-time core jobs but they are compelled
to compete with part-time workers for jobs in the penumbra.

This emphasis on the changing structure of the British economy suggests that we should use a structural approach to explain the rise of
youth unemployment. However, it is unlikely that any one economic
model will provide a completely satisfactory explanation of the behaviour
of the actual market for young labour at all times. Each approach offers
some valuable insights which aid our understanding of the causes of
youth unemployment. Although the three models are inconsistent with
each other in some respects, it might be still possible to devise a set
of practical and consistent policies to reduce youth unemployment based
on parts of the models. The neo-classical emphasis on the high relative
wages of young people making them too expensive to be trained is quite
consistent with a Keynesian policy of targeted demand increases to
reduce youth unemployment in our dilapidated inner cities, and neither

policy would be undermined by proposals to adjust the tax and national insurance system in the structuralist approach. Thus both price and quantity adjustments may be needed to decrease youth unemployment. Neo-classical economists recommend the stick of reductions in relative wages. Keynesians offer the carrot of increases in aggregate demand. Structuralists advocate the removal of market barriers which hinder the operation of both neo-classical and Keynesian policies. The approach of the present book is essentially pragmatic; it uses all three models to formulate policies to reduce youth unemployment. None of the proposals makes a serious dent in the protective belt surrounding the hard core of any one of the scientific research programmes currently adopted and, therefore, should be acceptable to all schools of thought. Some of the measures may have only marginal effects individually, but when they are aggregated the resulting package should significantly improve the employment prospects of young people.

Actual policies are discussed in Chapter 9, and are based on the findings of earlier chapters. Chapter 2 summarises the statistics, Chapter 3 assesses the importance of relative wages on youth unemployment, and Chapters 4 and 5 deal with the supply and demand for young labour. Some check on these findings is provided by Chapter 6, which compares the British experience of youth unemployment with that in France and West Germany, and by Chapter 7, which surveys the market for young labour in one United Kingdom industry, retail distribution. Chapter 8 summarises the results of recent spatial analyses of unemployment which supplement the findings of earlier chapters based on time series. As far as possible, the more technical parts of each chapter are consigned to notes at the end of the book.

THE TIME SERIES OF YOUTH UNEMPLOYMENT

INTRODUCTION

This chapter reviews the time series of youth unemployment in Great Britain 1952–81; corresponding unemployment rates are not available for the period before 1952, and since 1981 the various Government schemes to reduce recorded youth unemployment make the estimates for more recent years non-comparable.[1] However, the 30 annual observations available constitute a time series which is long enough to reveal any deterministic trend, and any structural breaks. We can also provide a summary of changes in youth unemployment since 1980, using the non-comparable data excluded from the analysis.

THE UPWARD TREND

Let us begin with charts 2.1 and 2.2 which are based on Wells (1983) and show unemployment rates (including school leavers) for young males and females separately for 1952–85 on an absolute scale.[2] The series for under twenty year olds has been used in the past to measure youth unemployment in Great Britain, although the usual definition of young in the European Community is less than 25 years, as explained in Appendix 1. The British and the broader European definitions are used later in this chapter to measure youth unemployment since 1980, even though the numerous changes in the official statistics since then make this updating somewhat hazardous. Unemployment rates of those under eighteen years, and hence for those under twenty years, are heavily affected by Government measures, such as the Youth Opportunities Programme since 1979 and the Youth Training Scheme and the Young Workers' Scheme since 1981. Perhaps a less misleading extrapolation may be obtained by confining attention to the 18–19 year olds, omitting the 16–17 year olds (including those on YTS) from both the numerator and denominator of the unemployment rate. This is done in charts 2.1 and 2.2 using table 2.2. The most recent data reveal a downswing from the peaks of 1983 and 1984, but this might be a cyclical fall similar to that in 1977–79 rather than a reversal of the upward trend. Since the latest data provide little extra information about the trends, we may confine the formal analysis to the comparable unemployment rates 1952–81.

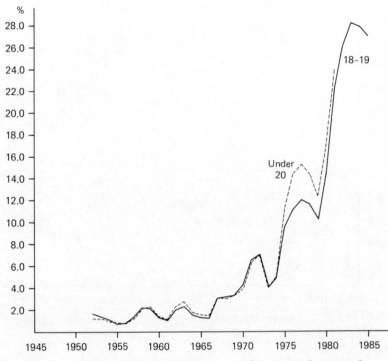

Chart 2.1 Estimated unemployment rates by age: males 1952–85

It is clear that there is not one linear upward trend throughout the whole period. But it could be argued that there were linear upward trends for both males and females up to 1973, and that afterwards there were much steeper linear upward trends in both series. It would not be difficult to regard 1973, the last year before the OPEC oil price increases, as indicating a structural break in the time series. However, when Merrilees and Wilson (1979) and Wells (1983) estimated their econometric models of the market for young labour, using disequilibrium techniques, they concluded that there was a structural break in 1969 for young males, and in 1971 for young females, when there was a switch from excess demand for young labour to an excess supply.

An alternative approach is followed in the present chapter and the logarithm of the youth unemployment percentage is plotted in charts 2.3 and 2.4 for males and females under twenty years of age.[3] These unemployment rates, like many other economic time series, exhibit variation which increases in mean and dispersion over time in proportion to the absolute level of the variable. The logarithmic transformation

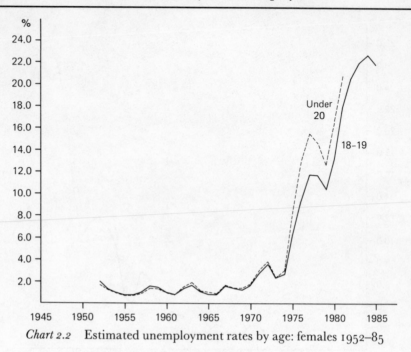

Chart 2.2   Estimated unemployment rates by age: females 1952–85

certainly graduates the data very well; the cycles and upward trend are clearly seen. But there is no obvious structural break although it could be argued that even after logarithmic transformation the upward trend is non-linear, accelerating after 1973, especially for females.

Charts 2.3 and 2.4 also facilitate a comparison between the unemployment rates for those under twenty and those twenty years or more. After 1962 the rates for young people were always higher than those for adults. This is consistent with the theory that young people tend to have higher unemployment rates because they spend more time searching for jobs. However, the fact that youth unemployment rates were sometimes lower than adult rates before 1962 is inconsistent with this theory although prior to 1962 all the rates were low.

A trend term contains all the systematic forces excluded from the model of unemployment being used but which appear to influence it in the longer run. These forces may act additively, in which case the percentage unemployment would be used as a dependent variable, or they may act multiplicatively so that the logarithm of the unemployment percentage would be used. In either case the measurement of the trend is an exercise in economic history rather than in forecasting.[4] It is a useful preliminary to an explanation of why each peak of unemployment

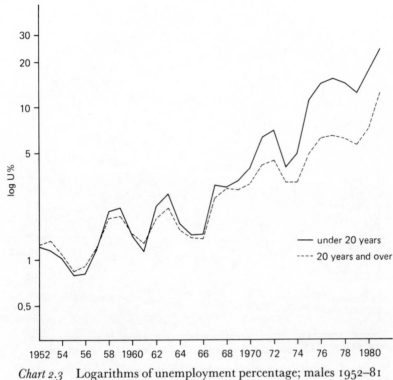

Chart 2.3   Logarithms of unemployment percentage; males 1952–81

exceeds the previous one. While it is true that an extrapolation of an upward trend in the unemployment rate would reach 100 per cent sooner or later, this frightening result merely indicates the dangers of extrapolation outside the observational period rather than the limitations of measuring such a trend within the observational period.[5]

It is always possible to dispute the existence of any upward trend in youth unemployment by selecting a plausible explanatory variable which also has a strong upward trend, so that after its influence on youth unemployment is removed in a regression analysis no trend remains. Such an explanatory variable might be the wages of youths relatively to adults, as in Wells (1983). He also includes the logarithm of the aggregate male unemployment rate as an explanatory variable which is known to have an upward trend. His dependent variable is the logarithm of the employment of young labour and since he uses the first differences of the logarithms of variables, his constant terms provide a measure of the trend; the constant terms are either not significantly different from zero or they are significantly below zero. The downward trend in the logarithm of youth employment is consistent with

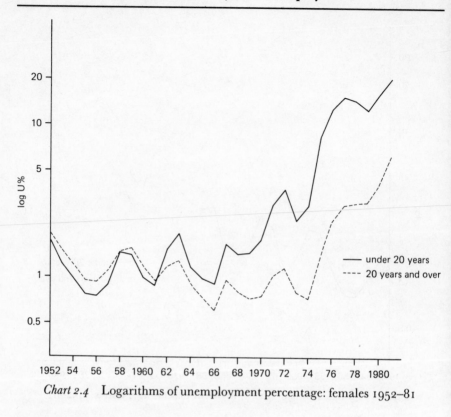

Chart 2.4   Logarithms of unemployment percentage: females 1952–81

an upward trend in the logarithm of youth unemployment. Moreover, the absence of statistically significant trends might be the result of having very few observations, especially in his sub-periods. The interesting result is that none of his demand for labour equations has a significant downward trend and that whenever such a trend emerges it is in his supply of labour equations. The upshot is that there is an upward trend in youth unemployment, even after removing the influence of relative wages and of the worsening trade cycle, and that the explanation of Wells (1983) emphasises supply-side rather than demand-side factors. Additional support for the existence of an upward trend in youth unemployment is provided by Appendix 3 on aggregate unemployment.

The causes of the long-term increase in youth unemployment are even more complex than the causes of the upward trend in adult unemployment. Some of the explanations advanced for the upward trend in aggregate unemployment may be relevant but others may not apply to youth unemployment. There is no shortage of possible explanations of the upward trends of unemployment in general and in youth unemployment in particular. Chapters 3, 4 and 5 survey the evidence on possible explanations in the context of the traditional economic model of the supply, demand and wages of young labour. But before studying the research on the effects of relative wages on youth employment in Chapter 3, it is necessary to examine the time series of youth unemployment rates to see whether it has the structural breaks suggested by the disequilibrium econometric models used to show that increases in relative wages have produced increases in youth unemployment.

STRUCTURAL BREAKS

Much of the high level of youth unemployment has the same causes as does adult unemployment. Indeed Makeham (1980) argued that changes in youth unemployment are so closely associated with changes in overall unemployment, albeit with greater amplitude, that there is no need to introduce other hypotheses (such as exceptional pay increases or unemployment benefits) as an explanation of changes in youth unemployment. That is, whatever economic model explains the aggregate male unemployment rate, U, also explains the youth unemployment rate, U_{YM}. In particular, U_{YM} and U have similar cycles and trends, so that the effects of the cycle and trend on U_{YM} may be removed by a regression of U_{YM} on U. However, the regression of the male youth unemployment percentage on total male unemployment percentage reported by Makeham increased from 1.66 in the period 1959–76, to 1.88 for 1959–80. This upward movement in the regression coefficient suggests that additional factors influence youth unemployment.

A formal method of investigating the changing regression relationship between youth unemployment, U_{YM}, and adult male unemployment, U_{AM}[6], is based on the recursive least squares residuals.[7] Using all 30 observations 1952–81 we have

$$U_{YM} = -1.95 + 2.31\,U_{AM}, \qquad \overline{R}^2 = 0.95 \qquad \text{2.1}$$
$$(0.39)\ (0.09)$$

Using the first three observations 1952–4, the coefficients become 0.275 and 0.0704; using the first four observations, they become 0.069 and 0.869. Observations are added until all 30 are used to get equation 2.1. The time series of regression coefficients thus obtained can be inspected for structural breaks. Furthermore, a sequential Chow test may be used to test for a structural change in the regression coefficients, as shown by Harvey (1976).

These tests are applied to the regression of log U_{YM} on log U_{AM} in view of the logarithmic relationship between youth and adult unemploy-

Table 2.1. *Sequential Chow tests for structural breaks (log-linear)*

	Structural breaks
Chow 1	1968, 1974, 1975, 1981
Chow 2	1967/8, 1975/6
Chow 3	1973/5

ment in charts 2.3 and 2.4. The two series for females have no obvious trends before 1967 for those under twenty, or before 1974 for those over twenty, and their rapid increase after these dates may be due in part to the increased propensity of women to register as unemployed. No such shortcoming applies to the series for males in chart 2.3, and because of this, the more detailed analysis of the relationship between youth and adult unemployment is confined to males.

Table 2.1 reports the results of sequential Chow tests on the forward regression of log U_{YM} on log U_{AM} starting with the window of three observations 1952–4 and adding observations in blocks of one, two, three, and so on. These tests revealed significant changes in the regression relationship in 1968, 1974, 1975, and 1981 when an extra observation was added, shown in row 'Chow 1'. When blocks of two observations were added, significant breaks occurred in 1967/8 and 1975/6, and when blocks of three observations were added there was one significant break in 1973/5. When blocks of more than three observations were added, only one significant break occurred and the period of change included the 1974 break. Adding blocks of only one, or even two, observations allows freak observations or 'outliers' to influence the results. The risk of such an effect is reduced by using blocks of three.

This supports the belief that after 1973 there was a 'bend in the trend' of log U_{YM}. The conclusion to draw is that whatever forces were producing an upward log-linear trend in youth unemployment in the 1950s, 1960s and early 1970s were accentuated after 1973. If it is desired to measure the working of the youth labour market in two separate periods, the appropriate break seems to be 1974, rather than the 1969 adopted by Merrilees and Wilson (1979) and Wells (1983). This result has important implications for the disequilibrium models of the relationship between youth employment and relative wages discussed in Chapter 3. Meanwhile the present discussion of the time series is continued in the next section by a summary of the data available in recent years.

YOUTH UNEMPLOYMENT IN RECENT YEARS

The numerous changes in the official statistical definitions of unemployment since 1980 make it very difficult to continue the time series of

Table 2.2. *Unemployment rates for 18–19 year olds (per cent)*

	Males		Females	
	GB (Wells)	UK (July)	GB (Wells)	UK (July)
1980	14.3	14.5	13.3	13.3
1981	22.2	21.9	17.9	17.4
1982		26.2		20.6
1983		28.2		22.0
1984		27.9		22.7
1985		27.1		21.8

Sources: Great Britain: Wells (1983), table D.17, page 95. United Kingdom: *Employment Gazette*, June 1986, table 2.15, page 537. Rates before and after October 1982 are not comparable due to changed methods of counting. Even before 1982 the time series used by Wells (1983) were reduced by the exclusion of youngsters on the Youth Opportunities Programme (increasing from 95,000 in 1979 to 240,000 in 1981), although the numbers excluded were less than those currently on YTS and YWS 404,000 in 1985.

youth unemployment compiled by Wells (1983). Table 2.2 gives the official estimates of unemployment rates of 18–19 year olds since 1980 used to extrapolate the Wells series in charts 2.1 and 2.2. The close correspondence between the two series for 1980–81 might justify this extrapolation.

Table 2.3. shows the rates of unemployment and of part-time working of young people aged 16–19 years and 20–24 years based on the Labour Force Survey. More details are given in Appendix 4 but it must be noted here that those on government schemes, such as the Youth Training Scheme (YTS) and the Community Programme, are included in the employed. It can be seen that youth unemployment rates reached a peak in 1983 for the 16–19 year olds and then fell to 1985. For 20–24 year olds the peak unemployment rate was reached in 1984. Table 2.3 also shows that part-time employment rates increased from 1979 to 1985 for males and females in each age group; some of the unemployed appear to have taken part-time jobs. If the unemployed and part-timers are added together to reflect the excess of the supply of labour over demand, it is clear that the upward trend continued until 1984. But the 1985 figures, which are still provisional, indicate a slight decrease from 1984.

Thus youth unemployment remains a very serious problem, notwithstanding the Youth Training Scheme and the Special Employment Measures. The redeeming feature usually cited is that, unlike unemployment among older workers, youth unemployment tends to be of short duration. As shown by table 2.4, some 52 per cent of unemployed people under 25 years had been out of work for less than six months in July

Table 2.3. *Unemployment and part-time rates for young people, Great Britain,*
1979–85 (Spring) (per cent)

	1979	1981	1983	1984	1985
Age 16–19 years					
Males U	12.8	23.1	24.7	22.1	20.2
P	3.4	9.3	9.2	13.1	13.5
Females U	14.3	20.8	21.0	20.1	17.9
P	6.9	15.4	18.0	21.1	23.0
Age 20–24 years					
Males U	6.7	15.7	18.8	18.8	17.3
P	0.7	1.0	1.6	2.3	3.3
Females U	8.7	12.4	13.4	14.8	13.4
P	8.9	8.6	9.2	11.8	12.5

Source: Appendix 4.
Note: U = unemployed, P = part-time.

Table 2.4. *Duration of youth unemployment (incomplete spells), Great Britain,*
July 1986

Duration	Percentage of unemployed youth		
	Under 20 yrs	20–24 yrs	Under 25 yrs
less than 6 months	57.4	48.3	52.0
6 to 12 months	24.1	18.9	21.0
12 to 24 months	14.0	14.3	14.1
24 to 36 months	3.8	7.2	5.9
36 months and more	0.7	11.3	7.0

Source: *Employment Gazette*, September 1986, p. 527, table 2.6.

Nevertheless, 27 per cent had been unemployed for more than a year, with 7 per cent without a job for more than three years.

The severity of the problem is also illustrated in table 2.5 which compares youth unemployment in 1931 and 1985. Although the two sets of unemployment rates are not exactly comparable, the estimates for 1985, especially for teenagers, appear to be even higher than in 1931 despite counting all those on special schemes as employed and making no allowance for the increase in part-time working. For males, the all-ages unemployment rate derived from the Census of Population 1931 was 12.7 per cent, thus the unemployment rates for those under twenty years were below the average. The same was true for females since the average

Table 2.5. *Unemployment rates for young people in England and Wales 1931 and Great Britain 1985 (per cent)*

	1931			1985	
Age	Males	Females	Age	Males	Females
14–15	4.9	5.0			
16–17	7.6	6.8	–	–	–
18–20	11.5	8.2	16–19	20.2	17.9
21–24	14.5	9.1	20–24	17.3	13.4
All ages	12.7	8.6	All ages	15.5	9.7

Sources: 1931: Census of England and Wales 1931, General Report, page 157; 1985: Department of Employment *Gazette* (1985) June, p. 523 for all ages percentage on May 9th 1985, including school-leavers. Percentages for 16–19 and 20–24 years from table 2.3.

was 8.6 per cent. Nowadays, youth unemployment rates are even higher than the aggregate unemployment rates.

CONCLUSION

The discussion of the time series of youth unemployment in Great Britain in 1952–81 has emphasised the long-term increase rather than the short-term fluctuations. It found that even after logarithmic transformation, there are structural breaks, the main one occurring in 1974 after the first OPEC oil-price increase. Recent changes in youth unemployment do not alter this picture.

What were the main causes of the upward drift in youth unemployment? In this study we emphasise the systematic forces influencing this trend, although an alternative approach is mentioned in Appendix 3. The systematic force which has been studied most intensively in the past is the relative wage of young people. The evidence is reviewed in the next chapter.

3

YOUTH UNEMPLOYMENT AND RELATIVE WAGES IN THE UNITED KINGDOM: A SURVEY OF THE EVIDENCE

INTRODUCTION

This chapter is concerned with one possible explanation of youth unemployment, namely that the wages of young people are too high relatively to those of adults to enable the labour market to provide jobs for all those young people who need them. Let us consider seven recent studies which measure the relationship between youth employment and relative wages in the United Kingdom, namely Merrilees and Wilson (1979), Wells (1983), Hutchinson, Barr and Drobny (1984), Abowd, Layard and Nickell, (1981), Lynch and Richardson (1982), Rice (1986), and Junankar and Neale (1985). A more detailed discussion of the first six, including a summary of the difference between an equilibrium and a disequilibrium model, is published elsewhere by Hart (1986a).

Those who believe that the steep rise in youth unemployment is caused by increases in their relative wages may cite the *prima facie* evidence of Wells (1983) in table 3.1, which shows an astonishing increase in the *minimum wage rates* of sixteen and seventeen year old males relatively to those of adults in national agreements in the private sector 1966–82. However, the increase in the later years is not confirmed by the time series of relative *wage earnings* taken from the New Earnings Survey, which is also summarised by Wells (1983) and is reproduced in chart 3.1. This shows that the earnings of young males and females did not increase relatively to those of adult males between 1974 and 1982. This is important: unlike the data from the October Inquiry which are also plotted in chart 3.1, the New Earnings Survey covers services, distribution and non-manual labour and is more representative of the earnings of young people. However, neither series could be used to explain the massive increase in youth unemployment after 1974 shown in charts 2.1 and 2.2 of Chapter 2.

MERRILEES AND WILSON (1979)

This discussion paper has been very influential even though the authors have yet to publish it and were careful to state that it represents work

Table 3.1. *Percentage of adult rates paid to young workers in a sample of private sector national agreements: males 1966–82*

	15 year old	16 year old	17 year old
1966	42.4	48.9	57.4
1967	40.9	47.2	55.4
1968	41.8	48.1	56.5
1969	42.2	48.1	59.2
1970	43.6	49.9	62.8
1971	45.7	52.5	62.8
1972	44.2	50.8	60.7
1973	45.8	51.0	61.3
1974	—	56.1	65.7
1975	—	57.0	67.4
1976	—	56.5	66.7
1977	—	58.3	68.6
1978	—	56.4	66.8
1979	—	60.2	70.8
1980	—	60.0	70.9
1981	—	60.3	71.7
1982	—	60.2	71.7

Source: Wells (1983), table 8, p. 23.

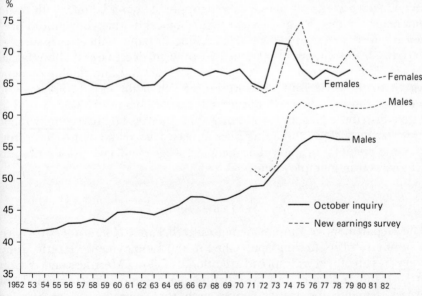

Chart 3.1   Weekly earnings of young people relative to adults.
Source: Wells (1983) table 1, p. 5, table D2, p. 81. (Male adults over 21 years, female adults over 18 years.)

in progress. In particular its disequilibrium approach and its sample separation have been adopted by Wells (1983) and underpin his important conclusion that the relative increase in the average earnings of young people under eighteen reduced their employment in the period 1969–81.

Merrilees and Wilson (1979) separate their sample period 1952–78 into period 1, 1952–69 for males and 1952–71 for females, when they claim there was excess demand for young labour, and the subsequent period 2 when they claim there was an excess supply.[1] Using annual data and the first differences in the natural logarithms of variables, they present estimates of the supply equation for young males and females for period 1. But why did not the relative wages of young labour rise sufficiently in period 1 to remove the excess demand postulated by the authors? Was it because trade unions wanted to preserve youth-adult wage differentials? Until some explanation is provided we must be reluctant to accept the estimated supply equations.

The authors then estimate an employment function for the whole period 1952–78 in which the supply variable operates only in the first sub-period and the demand variables operate only in the second sub-period. The dependent variable is the logarithm of the ratio of teenage to adult employment and the coefficients on relative wages have the correct negative sign and are significantly different from zero. These are interesting results for it is easier to accept the assumption that the second sub-period was one of excess supply of young labour, with trade union agreements, Wage Council regulations and other conventions preventing teenage money wages from falling to remove the excess supply. Perhaps trade unions also wished to prevent decreases in the relative wages of young people, thus avoiding increases in adult unemployment which might arise from substitution of young for older workers. For policy purposes, it is worth noting that the authors used a wage variable with a distributed lag and found that the response of relative employment to it was very slow, spreading over at least four years. Thus, according to these results, cutting young people's wages will take a long time to remove youth unemployment.

WELLS (1983)

The Department of Employment Research Paper No 42, together with a summary of its findings published in the Employment Gazette, June 1983, has attracted widespread attention. It follows Merrilees and Wilson (1979) and separates the observation period into two sub-periods of excess demand and excess supply with 1969 marking the change for young males and 1971 marking the change for young females.

Against this Chapter 2 shows that sequential Chow tests do not reveal the structural break in 1969 which might be expected if a switch between excess demand and excess supply occurred then. On the other hand, Wells found that there was a structural break in his supply equation for males in 1969.

Another reason for the structural break in 1969 advanced by Wells is that two Triennial Reports of the Youth Employment Service for 1965–8 and 1968–71 allude to buoyant markets for young labour whereas a report for 1971–4 was more gloomy about the prospects for young people. However the fact that the chances of getting a job were smaller in the 1970s than in the 1960s could be explained by the general economic depression following the OPEC oil price increases and certainly does not imply that there had been excess demand for young labour in the 1950s and 1960s. It is also argued that the alternative explanation is that the market for young labour was in equilibrium, which lacks credibility. But those who use an equilibrium approach do not claim that the labour market is, or has been, in equilibrium, they merely postulate that there are tendencies to bring about equilibrium. The general conclusion to draw from the evidence is that the *a priori* case for sample separation, in particular for choosing 1969 and 1971 as switching years, is not proven, and this is admitted by Wells.

Does this mean that it is safe to ignore the regressions obtained for the earlier period, especially when apparently significant supply-side coefficients have been estimated? Unlike Merrilees and Wilson, Wells found significant positive effects of wages on the supply of labour for both males and females in the earlier period, which is interesting. Less interesting is the highly significant elasticity of unity on *PPOP*, the potential population (that is, total young population less those in education or in the armed forces), for this only differs from the dependent variable by a relatively small amount. It is not surprising that when a variable is virtually regressed upon itself a significant coefficient of near unity emerges, and this probably explains most of the relatively high values of $\bar{R}^2$ obtained. Thus on balance very little useful information is lost if the equations for the earlier period are omitted, especially when no convincing reasons can be found to explain why the earnings of young people did not rise to eliminate the alleged excess demand.

The argument that there was an excess supply of young labour in the later epoch is less difficult to sustain; it is reasonable to accept the hypothesis that money wages are rigid downwards, as the result of trade union resistance to wage cuts. It may also be difficult to reduce the relative wages of young people if differentials are jealously guarded. But it is very difficult to understand why changes in the relative pay of young people appear to have been so perverse. Perhaps one reason is that the reduction in the age of majority from 21 to eighteen years led to an increase in the proportion of eighteen year olds who, with a maximum of two years' work experience, received adult rates of pay even though the unemployment rate of young people was increasing so rapidly. Even more striking is the perverse movement of the relative wage rates of young people negotiated in the private sector. For example the negotiated rate for a sixteen year old in 1970 was 49.9 per cent of the adult wage rate and this percentage was *increased* to 57 by 1975, and to 60 by 1980 (table 3.1). It is clear that wage differentials were not rigid in this period: on the contrary, they moved sharply in the opposite direction needed to eliminate any excess supply of young labour.

With such perverse increases in the wages of young people, it is less surprising that Wells was able to obtain significant negative coefficients on current relative labour costs in his demand equations estimated for 1969–81. He was unable to repeat this for the 18–19 year olds and concluded that the excess supply of young labour was concentrated in the under eighteen years group. While some of these re-estimations of the demand equations of Merrilees and Wilson have econometric limitations, such as low $\bar{R}^2$ and possibly negative serial correlation, it would appear that the proportionate increase in the relative labour costs of young people reduced the proportionate increase in the demand for their labour over the period 1969–81.

Wells then reports estimates of demand equations for the second epoch based on models formulated by Abowd *et al.* (1981) and Hutchinson *et al.* (1979). He was usually able to obtain statistically significant effects of relative labour costs on employment, although the precise numerical value of the effect is uncertain. Considering the small number of observations available this uncertainty is not surprising.

ABOWD, LAYARD AND NICKELL (1981)

This working paper estimates a system of demand equations for labour of different types using a dual cost function[2] of transcendental logarithmic form.[3] It is firmly based on the neo-classical economic theory of a competitive firm with an output of a homogeneous product y, with inputs x_j $(j = 1, \ldots n)$ at input prices w_j.

The theoretical Slutsky symmetry conditions $\partial x_j/\partial w_k = \partial x_k/\partial w_j$ are imposed as restrictions in their estimation methods and may be interpreted as follows. Suppose j refers to young males and k refers to young females. Then the change in the number of young males employed following a unit increase in the wage rates of young females is the same as the change in the number of females employed following a unit increase in the wage rates of young males. If $\partial x_j/\partial w_k$ is positive, j and k are substitutes. If it is negative, they are complements. Thus in a labour market context, if young males are substitutes for young females, then young females are substitutes for young males.

Clearly this theory cannot be extended to the economy as a whole. Young males in the construction industry could be substituted for young females in retail distribution, but the latter are not normally substitutes for young males in construction.[4] The symmetry conditions do not hold for the economy as a whole because aggregate output is not homogeneous. Hence it might be wrong to estimate a system of demand for labour equations from aggregate data with these symmetry conditions imposed as restrictions.

In the theoretical model, short-run and long-run cost curves (marginal, average, total) must rise for the firm to reach equilibrium. Once again this condition might not hold in the short run for the economy as a whole. Furthermore, the falling factor demand curve in the model yields own-price factor demand elasticities which must be negative so that if wage rates are increased, the demand for labour falls. The extension of the result from the theory of a single firm to the whole economy in a time of severe economic depression has been challenged by some economists.

In the long run when all inputs are free to vary, the cost function for any given set of input prices w_j at any given output y is obtained by minimising $C = \Sigma_j w_j x_j$, subject to $y = f(x_1 \ldots, x_n)$. Since the production function does not contain w_j as an argument, it follows that $\partial C / \partial w_j = x_j$. This is used to obtain a demand equation for labour of the jth type (x_j) from the cost function C. They then multiply x_j by w_j / C to obtain the elasticity of total costs with respect to w_j which equals the share of the jth factor in total cost;

$$(\partial C / \partial w_j) \, (w_j / C) = w_j x_j / C \qquad 3.1$$

But statistical data on x_j or $w_j x_j / C$ reflect not only the demand for the jth factor, but also its supply. The fundamental problem of identification is not discussed by the authors. Since a time series of x_j is not necessarily a time series of the demand for labour, the observed data might not be appropriate.

Abowd, Layard and Nickell must be making an implicit assumption that they have identified demand equations and they proceed to estimate the required parameters by regressing $w_j x_j / C$ on the logarithmic derivative of the cost function, $\partial \log C / \partial \log w_j$, postulating that the transcendental logarithmic (or translog) cost function holds in the aggregate. They then estimate a system of demand equations applying a generalised least squares technique known as 'seemingly unrelated regressions' to time series data.[5] The first set of results shows negative own-price elasticities for men, women and youths. They find that, in terms of their labour, men are substitutes for women and for youths, but women and youths are complements. The authors then investigate alternative models with specified lags and also decompose labour into workers and hours per worker. The own-price elasticities are usually negative though not always significantly different from zero (for example, male workers in their table 5A). The own-price elasticity of hours with respect to hourly earnings is *positive* for men in their tables 4 and 6, but these elasticities are small and not significantly different from zero. Denoting the cross-price elasticity of factor i with respect to factor price j as e_{ij} it may be seen that e_{wy} and e_{yw} have different signs in their tables 4, 5A and 6 which conflict with their theory. These perverse results might be explained by the fact that the time series data also reflect the supply of labour and the estimation methods used do not in fact identify a system of demand equations. Another shortcoming is that the authors confine their estimates to manufacturing whereas the employment of young males and females is concentrated in non-manufacturing sectors, such as construction, distribution and services.

Nevertheless, Wells estimates labour demand equations based on their approach (after 'heavy tailoring'), and on the other studies surveyed here, for the period 1969–81. He finds a significant negative relationship between the demand for young male labour under eighteen and their labour costs relative to adult men. But no significant results emerge for other categories of young labour. He shows significant negative relationships between the demand for young males under eighteen and their labour costs relative to all females. The specifications used imply that young males are substitutes for female labour. At a later stage, he presents positive cross-wage elasticities confirming that young male labour is substitutable for that of adult men and of females.

HUTCHINSON, BARR AND DROBNY (1979) (1984)

The authors estimate a demand function for male labour under twenty years old using annual data over the period 1952–72 and single-equation regressions. In 1972 the National Insurance card count of employees ended, removing the prime source of data on age and employment. The dependent variable is L_{it} the actual employment level of young males in year t, and the explanatory variables include aggregate industrial production, time trends, average hours worked, wages relative to men and to female full-time and part-time workers. Time lags of up to three years are included in some equations.

Their preferred equation has an R^2 of 0.996 with a highly significant quadratic time trend and significant coefficients on manufacturing output (lagged two years), on lagged L_{1t} (one, two, and three years), youths' wages relative to men, to female full-time and part-time workers (all lagged two years). The coefficient on wages relative to men is positive whereas those on wages relative to women are negative. Hence the authors conclude that lads and men are complements whereas lads and women are substitutes. Clearly, these results are extremely interesting, but how reliable are they? A fundamental problem arises in the use of a single equation to summarise the youth labour market. If it is legitimate to assume that there is an excess supply of labour, a single demand equation may be identified. But the assumption of Hutchinson *et al.* that 1952–72 was a period of excess supply is most unlikely to be true. Some economists might argue that neither excess demand nor excess supply persisted throughout the period, and if that is correct a simultaneous equations model of the supply and demand for young male labour should be estimated. For example the highly significant time trend in L_{1t} must be influenced by supply-side factors such as the birth rate sixteen to twenty years previously and should not appear in a demand equation.

Nevertheless there are some interesting consistencies between their results and those of other researchers using somewhat different data and techniques. They find that there is at least a two-year time lag between an increase in relative wages and a reduction in the employment of young males. This seems to be rather long, but it is consistent with the findings of Merrilees and Wilson (1979). Their basic result that increases in relative wages have contributed to increases in youth unemployment is instructive. Again, Hutchinson *et al.* find that young male labour and female labour (full-time and part-time) are substitutes which is consistent with the results of Wells (1983) and of Abowd *et al.* (1981). However, their finding that young and adult male labour are complements is inconsistent with the results of the other papers.

LYNCH AND RICHARDSON (1982)

Using annual data 1950–78, the authors regressed the proportion of young unemployed to total unemployed on relative employment costs and on the supply of young workers. Measures reflecting business conditions were also included on the right-hand side and the regressions were performed for young males and females separately.

When male unemployment is used to measure general business conditions it was found that the employment costs of young workers relative to older workers had no significant effect on relative youth unemployment. The replacement ratio, measuring the effect of unemployment and social security benefits, was also found to be insignificant. However, when general business conditions were measured by total vacancies, instead of the total male unemployment rate, relative employment costs had a significant effect on youth unemployment: a 1 per cent increase in relative employment costs produced a 1.28 per cent increase in youth unemployment relative to total unemployment. The authors prefer this result and attribute the non-significance of relative employment costs in previous regressions to collinearity between the male unemployment rate and relative employment costs.

The regressions are repeated for young females and relative employment costs have a significant effect on the relative unemployment of young females irrespective of whether general business conditions are measured by the total female unemployment rate or by total vacancies. The relevant elasticity of unemployment with respect to relative labour costs is 2.52 for females compared with 1.28 for males. Thus increasing the relative labour costs of young women has an even larger effect on their relative employment.

The authors argue that the easiest way to reduce relative labour costs of young people, and thereby reduce their relative unemployment, would be to vary employers' national insurance contributions, lowering them for young workers and raising them for older workers. But they admit that their statistical results are 'open to discussion' and 'may well suffer to some degree from simultaneous equation bias'. This particular shortcoming is obvious from their mongrel regression equation which includes both demand and supply variables on the right-hand side. Furthermore, unlike Hutchinson *et al.* (1979) (1984), they make no allowance for time trends in spite of showing a clear upward trend in relative unemployment during the period 1950–78. The trend for females is steeper than that for males which may explain why they obtained higher elasticities for females than for males.

RICE (1986)

The author favours disequilibrium models, but she does not use prior sample separation into periods of excess demand and supply of young labour. Instead she relies on a maximum likelihood technique proposed by Maddala and Nelson (1974) to estimate both the parameters of the equations and the periods of excess demand and supply. Moreover, she rejects those disequilibrium models of the 'directional' or 'quantitative' type which include changes in prices (in this case wages) in the determination of the type and period of disequilibrium. Trade unions and wages councils ensure that the money wages of young labour are rigid downwards and it is reasonable to exclude negative wage changes from the model.

The author finds that there has been an excess supply of young male labour since 1972/3 and an excess supply of young female labour since 1971/2. This is consistent with the time series and is plausible enough to obtain widespread acceptance. The finding that there was an excess demand for young labour in the 1950s and 1960s, with a transitional phase in the late 1960s, is more controversial, because no reason is advanced to explain why wages were so rigid upwards or why the disequilibrium lasted for so long. A limitation of the particular disequilibrium model used is that no period of equilibrium can arise: there is no scope for disequilibrium in some periods and equilibrium in others.

In the demand constrained régime, the author concluded that relative earnings were responsible for a third of the increase in unemployment of young males between 1973/4 and 1977/8, compared with the effect of the general decline in demand which was responsible for half of the increase in this category of unemployment. Supply-side factors were responsible for less than 16 per cent of the increase in unemployment of young males and, in particular, social security benefits had no effect.

For young females, supply factors were more important and accounted for two thirds of the increase in their unemployment over the same period. In particular, a decline in the gap between their net earnings and benefits appears to have increased their participation in the labour force in the sense that more registered as unemployed in order to get the benefits. On the demand side, relative wages were responsible for 22 per cent of the increase in unemployment. The general fall in demand for output was responsible for 12.6 per cent of the increase in unemployment compared with 50.8 per cent in the case of young males. Presumably this difference is due in large part to the different industrial composition of the unemployment of young males and females with the latter concentrated in services and distribution which suffered less than manufacturing and construction from falling demand.

JUNANKAR AND NEALE (1985)

Before estimating their own disequilibrium model of the youth labour market, the authors pay special attention to the study by Wells. In particular, they re-estimated some of Wells' equations using a different measure of relative wages. Whereas Wells used data from the Department of Employment's October Inquiry until 1979 and estimated values for 1980 and 1981 by forward extrapolation based on regressing October Inquiry figures on the New Earnings Survey data 1971–9, Junankar and Neale reverse this procedure: that is, they use the regression of New Earnings Survey on October Inquiry data 1970–81 in backward extrapolation to obtain estimates for earlier years. For young females, the two series of relative wage costs are similar, but there are striking differences for young males.

So when the authors re-estimate Wells' equation for young males, no significant results emerge. In particular, there is no evidence that increases in relative wage costs reduce the employment of young males. But this conclusion is heavily dependent on their hypothetical data for relative earnings. Slightly better results are obtained for young females but the presence of serial correlation suggests that equations are misspecified.

The authors then estimate their own disequilibrium model, without prior specification of the periods and direction of disequilibrium in the youth labour market. They find that there was excess supply of young males 1960–81 and for females 1956–63 and 1974–81. The relative labour cost variable has no significant effect on the demand for young males but it does have a significant effect for females. Presumably, this different result for young males is explained by the very different behaviour of the series of their relative wage costs as constructed by Junankar and Neale.

CONCLUSION

From a technical point of view the seven econometric studies discussed here are impressive: disequilibrium models, dual transcendental logarithmic cost functions, dynamic diagnostics and many other sophisticated techniques have been used in attempts to relate youth unemployment to their relative costs of employment. The fact that the results are not always convincing is due to the inherent difficulty of measuring such economic relationships rather than to the inadequacy of available econometric techniques.

Six studies suggest that increases in the labour costs of young people relative to those of adults have been associated with increases in youth unemployment relative to that of adults, particularly in the 1970s and 1980s. The precise importance of relative labour costs compared with all the other determinants of youth unemployment has not been established, but for purposes of economic policy it is useful to know that there is widespread agreement among independent research workers that increases in relative wages have been one of the factors contributing to the high levels of youth unemployment.

However, all six base their key relative wage variable on data derived from the October Inquiry which is less representative of young people's wages than is the New Earnings Survey. When the latter data are used, as in the disequilibrium model in the seventh study, it is found that relative wage costs had no significant effect on the demand for young males, but they did have a significant effect on the demand for young females.

The New Earnings Survey is a more reliable guide to the behaviour of the wages of young people than is the October Inquiry because it covers distribution and services which have traditionally provided major points of entry for young people into the labour market. Unfortunately, this time series is not yet long enough for econometric analysis so a rigorous analysis of the effects of relative wages on youth employment cannot be undertaken. Meanwhile, we shall have to be content with less rigorous, non-econometric comparisons of relative juvenile-adult wage ratios for particular trades in West Germany and the United Kingdom as in Chapter 6. The cross-country observations on relative wages are few in number but they show larger variations than the time-series wage rates for the United Kingdom and hence provide useful information on the effects of relative wages on youth employment. But before discussing a cross-country comparison of relative wages, it is necessary to describe the long-term supply and demand forces at work in the market for young labour in Great Britain in order to improve our understanding of the causes of the long-term increase in youth unemployment. This is done in Chapters 4 and 5 using a descriptive rather than an econometric approach. Once again, the more technical matters are consigned to notes at the end of the book.

4

THE SUPPLY OF YOUNG LABOUR

INTRODUCTION

The supply of labour is heavily dependent on the growth of population. The study of the growth of the population features less prominently in economics now than at the time of Malthus but it is still necessary to examine these trends in order to show the changes in the supply of young labour, which probably had important effects on the labour market. This is done in the next section. It is convenient to follow this with a brief discussion of the supply of a substitute for young labour, namely married women part-time workers.

The supply of young labour is far from homogeneous. While there is room for debate on whether the average quality of school leavers has deteriorated in recent years, it seems clear that the dispersion of quality is too great for present labour markets and should be reduced by raising the standards of the low achievers. There is diminishing scope for employing ill-educated, unskilled youngsters in a world of rapid technological change and intense international competition. Lack of training may be a fundamental cause of our lack of competitiveness in world markets and thereby explain much of the increase in youth unemployment.

The supply of labour also partly depends on the real wage, (money wages deflated by an index of consumer goods prices such as the Retail Price Index). Money wages are sometimes defined as 'take-home pay', that is after deducting income tax and national insurance contributions. The aim is to estimate the real value of the wage that the marginal worker would be free to spend and which he would take into account before reaching a decision on whether to work. There is an extensive economic literature on the effects that the levels and changes in taxation, including national insurance contributions, have on the supply of labour through changing the real wage.

TRENDS IN THE SUPPLY OF YOUNG LABOUR

The trend in the growth of the population of young people indicates the growth in the *potential* supply of young labour. To put this growth into proper perspective, table 4.1 summarises the changes in the population of all ages and their employment from 1951 to 1981. The total home population increased by over 11 per cent with a 9.6 per cent increase

Table 4.1. *Long-term changes in population and employment, Great Britain, 1951–81 (millions)*

			Male	Female	Total
1.	Home population	1951	23.5	25.4	48.9
		1981	26.3	28.0	54.3
		Change	*2.8*	*2.6*	*5.4*
2.	Population of working age	1951	15.7	15.6	31.3
		1981	17.2	15.8	33.0
		Change	*1.5*	*0.2*	*1.7*
3.	Working population	1951	15.6	7.0	22.6
		1981	15.9	10.0	25.9
		Change	*0.3*	*3.0*	*3.3*
4.	Employees in employment	1951	13.4	6.5	19.9
		1981	12.2	9.0	21.2
		Change	*−1.2*	*2.5*	*1.3*
5.	Self-employed	1951	1.3	0.3	1.6
		1981	1.6	0.4	2.0
		Change	*0.3*	*0.1*	*0.4*
6.	Unemployed	1951	0.3	0.1	0.4
		1981	1.7	0.6	2.3
		Change	*1.4*	*0.5*	*1.9*
7.	HM Forces	1951	0.6	—	0.6
		1981	0.3	—	0.3
		Change	*−0.3*	*—*	*−0.3*
8.	Part-timers as % of total employment	1951	0.3	12.1	4.1
		1981	5.9	41.6	21.0
		Change	*5.6*	*29.5*	*17.2*

Sources: Rows 1 and 2: Annual Abstract of Statistics (1984), table 2.1, p.6. 1981 figures relate to 'persons present' and are not strictly comparable with 1951. Rows 3 to 7: 1951 British Labour Statistics Historical Abstract 1886–1968, table 104, p. 198; 1981 Annual Abstract (1984), table 6.1, p. 109. Row 8: 1951 Matthews *et al.* (1982), table 3.15, p. 73; 1981 *Employment Gazette* (1983), December. Occasional Supplement table 3, p. 5.

in males of working age and hardly any increase in the number of females of working age. In spite of this, the male working population rose by only 2 per cent while the female working population increased by an extraordinary 43 per cent, though this was primarily an increase in part-time employment. The total unemployed increased by some two million, only partly because 1981 was a year of recession, unlike 1951. Insufficient information is available on hours of work of females in part-time employment to be sure about the changes in the quantity of labour measured in hours worked. However, with the reduction of the working week and the increase in holidays, the total number of hours worked probably decreased between 1951 and 1981, continuing the downward trend to

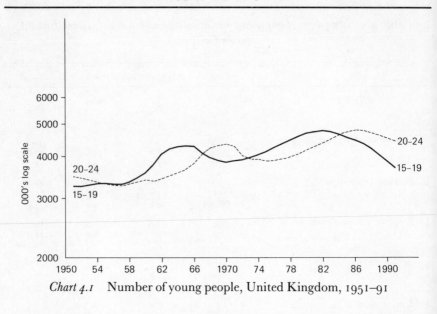

Chart 4.1 Number of young people, United Kingdom, 1951–91

1973 reported in Matthews *et al.* (1982, p. 265). Against this background
what happened to the supply of labour from young people?

Chart 4.1 shows mid-year estimates and projections of the young population 1951–91 on a logarithmic scale. The increasing numbers in the
15–19 and 20–24 years age groups are likely to have contributed to the
long-run upward trend in youth unemployment. Even more pronounced
are the shorter-run cycles stemming from earlier fluctuations in the birth
rate. The 15–19 age group reached peaks in 1965 and 1982, and the
20–24 age group in 1970 and 1987, so that demographic trends should
not increase youth unemployment in the next few years.

The time series in chart 4.1 are subject to revision although the broad
conclusions just discussed are unlikely to be altered. Estimates and projections of the young civilian labour force are shown in table 4.2. The
projected activity rates for females of 16–19 years show a fall between
1985 and 1991, after the increases since 1971. The male activity rate
for 16–19 year olds increased 1971–81 and is forecast to decrease until
1991. The activity rate for males aged 20–24 years is expected to be
much the same in 1991 as in 1983. These changes in activity rates applied
to population forecasts yield the net result that the 16–19 year old civilian
labour force will decrease from 2.53 million in 1983 to 2.03 million in
1991. But the 20–24 year olds reach a peak around 1987 before falling
to 1991. There will be a downward trend in the supply of young labour
after 1987.

For school-leavers, recent projections were published in the *Employment*

Table 4.2. *Recent and projected estimates of the young civilian labour force and their activity rates, Great Britain, 1971–91*

	Ages 16–19				Ages 20–24			
	Millions		Activity rate %		Millions		Activity rate %	
	M	F	M	F	M	F	M	F
1971	1.05	0.95	69.4	65.0	1.84	1.24	87.7	60.2
1973	1.03	0.93	66.1	62.9	1.68	1.17	86.5	61.3
1975	1.01	0.92	62.5	59.7	1.65	1.18	86.4	63.9
1977	1.19	1.12	70.2	68.8	1.66	1.24	85.2	66.2
1979	1.31	1.24	73.0	72.0	1.74	1.31	86.7	67.7
1981	1.36	1.26	72.4	70.4	1.79	1.41	85.1	68.8
1983	1.33	1.20	69.6	66.7	1.86	1.47	84.1	68.2
1985	1.32	1.21	72.6	69.9	1.98	1.58	85.0	69.9
1987	1.27	1.16	72.4	69.4	2.01	1.59	85.4	70.4
1989	1.19	1.08	72.0	69.0	1.95	1.54	85.1	70.2
1991	1.06	0.97	71.6	68.7	1.87	1.48	84.9	70.4

Source: Employment Gazette, July 1985, pp. 258–9.

Gazette, September 1986. Their numbers are expected to fall from 840,000 in 1986/7 to 680,000 in 1990/91. Most of this decline (some 120,000) is expected to take place for those available for employment. The numbers entering full-time further education are expected to decrease by 40,000. Government measures such as the Youth Training Scheme will also reduce recorded unemployment in the age range 16–18 years, but whether such intervention in the labour market merely postpones unemployment until the age of eighteen remains to be seen. Hopefully, training provided under the scheme will improve the quality of the supply of young labour which should improve their chances of obtaining employment. The training of young people is discussed later in this chapter. Meanwhile, let us consider the supply of substitute labour.

THE SUPPLY OF SUBSTITUTE LABOUR

The employment prospects of young people are likely to be affected by the supply of substitute labour. An indication of the scope for substitution is given by table 4.3 which compares the age, sex and industrial distribution of the occupied population[1] in 1951 and 1981. Corresponding tables for 1961, 1966 and 1971 are given in Appendix 5.

One trend which might improve the employment prospects of young people is the decrease in the number of men working beyond the age of 60 years. It can be seen that between 1951 and 1981 the male occupied population in this age group fell from 1.53 million to 1.16 million. But the declining sectors of agriculture, energy, manufacturing and transport lost about 370,000 men over 60 years between 1951 and 1981 and it

Table 4.3. *Occupied population by age, sex and industry, Great Britain, 1951 and 1981 (thousands)*

		Age 15	16–19	20–24	25–59	60+	All ages
1951							
Agriculture	a	19	88	104	667	133	1,011
	b	2	16	18	68	11	115
	c	21	104	122	736	144	1,126
Energy	a	10	58	92	890	103	1,153
	b	1	9	11	24	1	45
	c	11	67	103	914	104	1,198
Manufacturing	a	95	348	538	4,203	555	5,740
	b	94	467	445	1,515	77	2,597
	c	189	815	983	5,718	632	8,337
Construction	a	22	115	155	947	109	1,348
	b	1	8	9	21	1	40
	c	23	124	164	968	110	1,388
Transport and communications	a	10	49	125	1,186	120	1,489
	b	4	33	44	128	7	215
	c	14	82	169	1,313	126	1,704
Finance	a	1	11	23	225	26	285
	b	3	37	33	72	5	150
	c	4	49	55	296	31	435
Distribution	a	27	80	128	1,105	181	1,521
	b	52	211	191	635	64	1,152
	c	79	291	319	1,740	245	2,674
Services	a	12	291	325	1,825	296	2,749
	b	26	235	331	1,718	194	2,505
	c	39	526	657	3,543	490	5,254
Not stated	a	0	1	1	7	3	12
	b	0	2	1	3	0	6
	c	1	3	3	10	3	19
Total all industries	a	197	1,041	1,491	11,054	1,525	15,309
	b	183	1,018	1,082	4,182	360	6,826
	c	380	2,059	2,574	15,237	1,885	22,135

Source: Census of Population, 1951 table 111.4; 1981, table 10A.
Note: a = male; b = female; c = male + female.

seems likely that such contraction was primarily due to market conditions and provided little scope for the substitution of older men by young people.

There would appear to be more scope for substitutability between young people and the adult female labour force which has been increasing so much. The increase in the female working population of some 3 million 1951–81 noted in table 4.1, was due in part to the changing demands for labour in different industrial sectors. Agriculture, energy and transport are traditionally employers of males rather than females and they contracted their labour force by some 1.3 million. The employment of

Table 4.3. (*Contd.*)

		Age 15	16–19	20–24	25–59	60+	All ages
1981							
Agriculture	a		37	43	282	63	425
	b		6	7	67	10	90
	c		43	50	349	73	515
Energy	a		31	63	491	31	616
	b		8	18	67	2	95
	c		39	81	558	33	711
Manufacturing	a		283	466	3,293	357	4,400
	b		181	255	1,292	66	1,794
	c		464	721	4,586	423	6,194
Construction	a		132	167	1,086	93	1,478
	b		12	15	94	7	128
	c		144	182	1,180	100	1,606
Transport and communications	a		49	107	959	92	1,206
	b		29	48	200	13	290
	c		78	155	1,159	105	1,496
Finance	a		45	117	716	82	960
	b		120	179	505	31	835
	c		165	296	1,221	113	1,795
Distribution	a		147	182	1,045	160	1,535
	b		195	198	1,110	102	1,605
	c		342	380	2,156	262	3,140
Services	a		207	339	2,211	273	3,029
	b		248	471	3,263	255	4,237
	c		455	810	5,474	528	7,266
Not stated	a		17	15	76	8	116
	b		15	11	42	10	78
	c		32	26	118	18	193
Total all industries	a		948	1,499	10,159	1,159	13,765
	b		814	1,202	6,640	496	9,152
	c		1,762	2,701	16,799	1,655	22,916

females is concentrated in the expanding sectors of finance, distribution and services which provided nearly 4 million extra jobs, nearly 3 million of them for females.

The manufacturing sector which provided 37.7 per cent of employment in 1951 but only 27 per cent in 1981 is no longer the most important source of work: that distinction now belongs to services. The decline of 2.1 million jobs in manufacturing was nearly balanced by the increase of 2 million in services, with 1.7 million of this increase going to females. This huge increase in female employment, when general unemployment increased from 373,000 to 2.3 million, 1951–81, did not apply to all

Table 4.4. *Ten most important occupations for female part-time workers, Great Britain, 1981*

			Female part-timers				
			1981	% of all employees		Weight of occupation in	
SIC	1980	Name	000s	1981	1951	1981 %	1951 %
1.	90722	Cleaners	441	75.9	45.6	2.8	1.3
2.	70551	Shop assistants	428	51.5	10.2	4.0	4.5
3.	60463	Clerks	411	18.6	3.1	10.5	6.2
4.	90683	Domestics	367	78.3	17.6	2.2	3.0
5.	60492	Typists	207	27.6	6.0	3.6	2.8
6.	20160	Nurses	197	33.8	7.7	2.8	1.3
7.	90661	Counterhands	137	63.7	22.6	1.0	0.2
8.	90652	Barmaids	85	67.5	20.0	0.6	0.2
9.	90662	Kitchenhands	76	67.9	27.0	0.5	1.0
10.	20119	Teachers	74	11.5	3.7	3.1	1.5
Total above ten			2423	37.2	11.1	31.0	22.0
All other occupations			994	6.9	2.3	69.0	78.0
All occupations			3417	16.3	4.2	100.0	100.0

Sources: 1981: Office of Population Censuses and Surveys (1984) Census of Population, *Economic Activity Tables*, London: HMSO; 1951: General Register Office (1957) *Occupation Tables* London: HMSO.

age groups. There was a fall of 387,000 (over 32 per cent) in the employ-ment of young women under twenty years and about half of this was reflected in the nearly eleven-fold increase in the unemployment of young women.[2] The remaining half was due to their increased participation in post-compulsory education.

Of course the increase in the *numbers* of employed adult women was much greater than the increase in the *quantity* of female labour because the percentage of part-time jobs for women increased by a factor of 3.4. Female part-time workers formed 41.6 per cent of the female labour force in 1981 compared with 12.1 per cent in 1951, as shown in table 4.1.[3] This relatively large number of part-time jobs for females is a pecu-liarity of the British economy; we have a larger percentage of female part-time workers than our competitors in Germany, France, Italy, Japan and the United States.[4] In Britain female part-time workers appear to have jobs which are done by full-time workers in other countries. The growth of adult female part-time workers has been most rapid in sectors such as distribution (discussed in detail in Chapter 7) and services, which are traditionally employers of young people. For example, table 4.4 shows that in 1981 female part-time workers formed 51.5 per cent of all shop assistants, compared with 10.2 per cent in 1951. This five-fold increase in the proportion of female part-time employees was exceeded by the six-fold increase among clerks (not retail) while domestic workers, typists, and nurses increased their proportions of female part-time workers more than four-fold. These occupations are traditionally major sources of employment for young people, especially young females.

TRAINING AND QUALITY

The supply of young labour is not homogeneous; natural ability varies between individuals. But this does not imply that the supply of good quality young people is fixed because natural ability can be improved considerably by appropriate training and education. At the very least, young workers should be taught to cope with the ever increasing complexity of capital equipment. Part of the secular increase in youth unemployment is probably attributable to the failure of our training schemes to meet the skill requirements of modern industry. Compared with Germany, Japan, Switzerland and Austria, the United Kingdom provides woefully inadequate training for its young people and it is not surprising that our competitiveness has been reduced.

The shortcomings of the British apprenticeship system have been known for many years, at least since the 1880s. For example, Phelps Brown (1959, p. 56) comments on the inadequacy of training in the last quarter of the nineteenth century,

'A people that could escape starvation only so long as it could sell its industrial exports in competitive markets had done little for the industrial training of its young people ... The gap was seen, the technical and trade schools of France and Germany showed it up, and the foundations of the City and Guilds Institute as a central examining body in 1880 had resulted in an Act of 1889 that empowered the new county councils to promote technical instruction, within the limits of a penny rate; though in deference to the trade unions' fears of a flooding of their market, it also said that such instruction should "not include teaching the practice of any trade or industry or employment"'.

In the 1930s, when unemployment was very high, there was still an excess demand for skilled labour which was serious enough to impede the rearmament programme (Peden (1979)). The shortage of skilled labour was even more pronounced in the Second World War, and yet the reluctance to undertake formal technical training continued.[5] Barnett (1986) provides extensive evidence on the traditional neglect of technical training in Britain and argues that it amounts to education for industrial decline. Moreover, even those who completed apprenticeships were not necessarily formally examined in their skills. Serving one's time, without a formal testing of ability, was still the norm.

Liepman (1960) and Williams (1957) showed that even by the 1950s the severe limitations of the British apprenticeship system had not been removed. However, a comparison of Williams (1957) and Phelps Brown (1959) shows one important long-term change in the relationship between the apprenticeship system and the supply of labour. Traditionally the number of apprentices was restricted by trade unions in an attempt to maintain the scarcity value, and hence the wages, of journeymen. But Williams (1957) argued that such restrictions, however common before 1914, were not important in the 1950s, except for the printing trade. The reason why relatively few apprenticeships were given was because employers found them to be unprofitable. In particular the obligation to provide a day release scheme was very expensive to the employer, especially when the total working week was reduced from 5.5 days to 5 days a week. To pay a week's wage for only four days' work, without any guarantee that the apprentice would stay with the firm after serving his time, demanded a social obligation which fewer and fewer firms were prepared to accept. Even now, in the 1980s, it is all too often the case that the first item of firms' expenditure to be cut is that of training. It may be short-sighted, but in the United Kingdom operational time-horizons are often very short.

The scale of the training problem may be measured in part by the proportions of labour with or without some kind of vocational qualification. Prais (1981) shows that 64.4 per cent of the British labour force had no vocational qualification 1974–8 compared with 33 per cent in West Germany. This large deficiency in the skills of our labour force compared with those of our German competitors is not the result of lower levels of German examination standards, as is clearly demonstrated by Prais and Wagner (1983). In fact, because many of our skilled workers with vocational qualifications are not formally examined, unlike their German counterparts, it is likely that the true skill differential is *under-estimated* by the difference between the proportions with vocational qualifications.

Although these comparisons refer to the stocks of labour around 1978, rather than to the flow of young labour into the labour force, the point still holds: one reason why the secular rise in youth unemployment in Britain has been much greater than in West Germany is that the quality of the labour supply in Britain is lower than in Germany. In a competitive world, with increasing sophistication of production, the scope for untrained labour diminishes. The present government's YTS, and other training initiatives, are belated attempts to raise the general level of skills required by the labour force. These schemes fall far short of the German system, and all too often provide work experience rather than systematic training, but at least they are steps in the direction required to improve the chances of young people getting jobs in the future.

The deficiency of training in Britain is summarised by Davis (1986).

Even in 1967, only 5.5 per cent of manufacturing employees were receiving training, and this figure declined to 2 per cent by 1985. Before the introduction of YTS, 30 per cent of boys and 40 per cent of girls leaving school entered jobs with no formal training. It is hardly unexpected that even those who eventually manage to obtain jobs become inefficient operators, with their machines having more breakdowns and more downtime than would be the case in Germany, according to the findings of Daly, Hitchens and Wagner (1985).

There are many reasons for the insufficient training of our labour force, but the relative cost is one of them. The pay of German apprentices relative to adults is lower than in the United Kingdom, as shown in Chapter 6. Thus the high relative pay of British youngsters may lie at the root of our high youth unemployment, but not because of the theories of the pricing of homogeneous labour underpinning the econometric equations of Chapter 3. It seems that the relatively high wages of young people in Britain discourage employers from training them. At the same time, products which require a high skill content are imported. In order to halt the deskilling of our production, we shall need more training for our young workers, and retraining for our adult workers, which should raise the quality of our labour force.

Lack of training is also attributed to the bias of our educational system against vocational training, and indeed, to the inadequate basic education received by the bottom 50 per cent of pupils in our schools. The traditional methods of educating these pupils do not enable them to undertake the training they require to cope with the increasingly complicated methods of production in an increasingly competitive world. These important issues are discussed in Chapter 9 on policies to reduce youth unemployment.

THE EFFECTS OF TAXES AND BENEFITS

Many economists have attempted to measure the effects of taxation, particularly income tax, on the supply of labour. Unfortunately, as shown in a survey by Brown (1980), the reliability of the conclusions is not great, certainly not as great as the ingenuity shown in reaching them. The evidence is based on interviews, econometric studies and on five American experiments with negative income taxes. A more recent survey by Ashworth (1982) reviews the standard neo-classical theory of labour supply and summarises two sets of empirical results, one set relating to six interview studies of labour supply and the other to 23 econometric studies. The interview studies are summarised readily enough: a small minority of people claim that taxes are a *disincentive* to increasing labour supply (between 10 and 18 per cent of respondents) and another small minority claim that taxes are an *incentive* to increasing it (between 10 and 15 per cent). Thus most respondents (between 67 and 80 per cent) are unable to state whether taxes affect the provision of their labour. Bearing in mind all the limitations of interview surveys, it is nevertheless clear that for most people the effect of income tax rates on their decisions to work is not a burning issue.

The effects of taxes and benefits on the supply of young labour are difficult to model. First, let us consider the supply of young labour from those already in work. It may be assumed that most young earners are in the lowest income-tax band, for relatively few will be below the income tax threshold and even fewer below the age of twenty will earn enough to enter the higher tax bands. Thus the typical young worker will not encounter high marginal tax rates if he or she decides to increase his or her supply of labour by, for example, working overtime. In short, the relevant budget constraint in the standard theoretical income–leisure trade-off is likely to be linear. But this does not mean that the simple theoretical income–leisure trade-off model can be applied to young labour. In particular, most young people, like most adults, are obliged to work overtime if their firms have to meet urgent orders. This obligation stems explicitly from their contracts or is part of the customary practices which keep the plant going. That is, hours of work are probably influenced more by the demand for labour than by the supply.

In any case, the variation in labour supply most relevant to a study of youth unemployment depends on the original decision to enter the labour force which is a zero/one dependent variable. Econometric labour equations estimated from variation in the hours of work of *employed* people and the variations in tax rates are obviously unsatisfactory because they exclude all the unemployed (voluntary and involuntary) from the sample information.

In practice the participation decision is not always freely determined by young people. They are usually (90 per cent) secondary workers living with their parents and the household income is normally heavily dependent on the earnings of the primary worker, usually the father. There may be strong parental pressure on the teenager to compel him or her to seek work, even if the short-term financial gains are very small or even if they are negative. No doubt the conventional work ethic and distaste for laziness are important, but equally important are the longer-term effects of short-term voluntary unemployment. It is much easier for an employed than an unemployed teenager to obtain a new job. The prospective employer uses the fact of present employment as a screen; he does not know the actual capabilities of a youngster and since he does not have time to carry out exhaustive tests required to forecast them, he adopts the simple solution of assuming that an employed applicant, who has already been successful in his job search, is superior. This is well known to the typical parent, who for this reason would himself normally seek another job without having an intervening spell of unemployment. It is equally well known to the teenager: the first job is always the hardest to obtain and it is wiser to accept it as a stop-gap until something better is offered rather than to reject it, especially in times of high unemployment. Furthermore, there is always the possibility that such a job will open the door to a better post within the same firm, once the teenager has a chance to demonstrate his worth.

The counter argument is that while the income–leisure trade-off theory does not apply to the typical young person (after all, most of them are in work or continuing their education), it might provide valuable insights into the behaviour of the atypical young person who is most likely to be unemployed. Suppose his family does not accept the conventional work ethic, suppose his parents are unemployed and have a detailed knowledge of the rules for obtaining unemployment and other benefits, then he might well continue the parental tradition and decide not to participate unless there is a large excess of net wages over benefits, costs of travel to work and so on. Furthermore, voluntary youth unemployment might also arise because young unemployed people prolong the length of search for jobs, fortified by social security benefits, in a vain attempt to obtain work at excessively high wages: their expectations are too ambitious.

These theoretical arguments are interesting but what are the facts? Since a typical unemployed young person does not have the national insurance contribution record to obtain unemployment benefit, he or she has to rely on supplementary benefit. The ordinary supplementary benefit rate of a 16–17 year old living in another person's household was raised to £18.20 a week for 1986. A 16 year old who refuses to join the Youth Training Scheme has a deduction of 40 per cent for up to six weeks. The ordinary supplementary benefit of an 18–20 year old single non-householder was £23.60 a week. Were these benefits so high that they generated voluntary youth unemployment?

Table 4.5 shows the real value of supplementary benefits of young people increased from 1959 to 1974 but since then, when the enormous rise in youth unemployment took place, it has been trendless. Makeham (1980) shows that even in the period before 1974 there was no tendency for the replacement ratios of young people, defined as their scale rates of supplementary benefit divided by their average net earnings, to increase. Furthermore, in his regressions of youth unemployment on adult unemployment, youth pay, youth population and real social security benefits, he found that the coefficients on the latter were not significantly different from zero. This result was later confirmed by Lynch

Table 4.5. *Real value of supplementary benefits of young people 1959–85, July (£s)*

	Scale SB			
	16–17	18–20	Average	adjusted for RPI
1959	1.30	1.58	1.44	2.98
1960	1.50	1.80	1.65	3.35
1965	2.23	2.58	2.40	4.08
1970	2.80	3.20	3.00	4.08
1974	5.15	6.70	5.93	5.40
1975	5.90	7.65	6.78	4.89
1980	11.25	14.65	12.95	4.83
1981	13.10	17.05	15.08	5.07
1982	14.30	18.60	16.45	5.09
1983	15.80	20.55	18.18	5.40
1984	16.50	21.45	18.98	5.40
1985	17.30	22.45	19.88	5.33
1986	18.20	23.60	20.90	5.42

Sources: P. Makeham (1980) Youth Unemployment, Department of Employment Research Paper No. 10. Table 22, p. 83. NIESR calculations for more recent years use same methods.
Notes: Scale rates of supplementary benefits for young people (defined as 'someone living in another person's household') from Social Security Statistics 1985. From 1974, the scale rate for those aged eighteen years and over was used for the 18–20 column. Adjustment for RPI based on January 1974 = 100.

and Richardson (1982) who found that the relative replacement ratio was never significant in their youth unemployment regressions and was therefore dropped from their basic model.

However, the more recent work by Rice (1986) discussed in Chapter 3 modifies these results. She found that in periods of supply constraint, when there is excess demand for young labour, increases in social security benefits lead to higher levels of voluntary youth unemployment. But in periods of demand constraint, when there is excess supply of young labour, increases in social security benefits do not lead to higher levels of voluntary youth unemployment. Instead, they tend to increase labour force participation rates (of young females rather than of young males) as more young women register as unemployed and formally signal that they have joined the labour force. Rice (1986) found that there was excess demand in the 1950s and early 1960s, but in the 1970s there was an excess supply of young labour. The absence of any effect of social security benefits on voluntary youth unemployment in the 1970s is consistent with the earlier results of Makeham (1980) and Lynch and Richardson (1982).

One of the most important differences between the results of Rice (1986) and those of earlier investigations relates to the causes of the increase in the unemployment of young males and young females in the 1970s. For young females, 'supply-side' factors including social security benefits were responsible for some two thirds of the increase in registered unemployment in the 1970s. But this did not hold for young males: 'demand-side' factors, mainly increases in their relative earnings and the low growth of output relative to their labour productivity, were responsible for over 80 per cent of the increase in registered male juvenile unemployment. Rice (1986) makes the plausible suggestion that these differences arise partly because juvenile males base their decisions on longer-term income streams and career structures rather than on short-term income (including social security) considerations, which appear to have greater influence on young females.

Another analysis of unemployment disaggregated by age is provided by Narendranathan et al. (1985), who found that the average effect of unemployment income on the expected duration of male unemployment is heavily concentrated among the young, being highest for young males aged 16–19 years. Their results indicate that for short-term unemployed teenagers a cut in real unemployment and social security benefits by 10 per cent would reduce the expected duration of their unemployment by 6.8 per cent or about 1.3 weeks on an average duration of 19.7 weeks. Although it is small, this elasticity is larger than that for older age groups. Indeed, for males aged 45–64 years, unemployment benefits had no significant effect on the duration of their unemployment.

Micklewright (1986) provides a most helpful survey of other recent research results on the effect of unemployment income on the supply of labour. For example, Lynch (1985) used a small sample of teenagers in London and found that benefits had no effect on their unemployment. But another paper, Lynch (1983), used a different model and found that benefits did have an effect on the duration of youth unemployment. This illustrates the extreme difficulty in obtaining firm results from statistical or econometric analysis of the relationship between benefits and voluntary unemployment. At most the effect is small and it is very difficult to measure.

In any case, there are clear limits to the power of statistical technique to measure the influences of benefits on youth unemployment. In particular, it cannot help us very much to assess the extent to which such unemployed youths participate in the black economy, which may well be important. That is, income tax may have an important effect on the supply of young labour at the margin by diverting it to the black economy where no taxes are paid. Unfortunately, the data required to measure this effect are not available.

But the increased participation of married women in the labour force is an influence which can be measured. They are potential substitutes for youngsters, particularly girls, and their decision to seek part-time work is likely to be influenced by taxation as well as by their domestic responsibilities. If they work sufficient hours in a week to earn £39 they are at present liable to pay national insurance contributions on the whole of their earnings. If they restrict their earnings to just under £39 per week or £2,028 per annum, they avoid national insurance contributions *and* income tax, for the wife's current earned income allowance is £2,425 per annum for the fiscal year 1987/8.

The increase in the married women's allowance to the single person's allowance dates from the Second World War when every effort had to be made to encourage married women to go out to work. Since 1942 two-earner married couples have enjoyed tax allowances of 2.5 times the single person's allowance. By the 1950s and 1960s, the tax thresholds were so low and the tax rates so high that they provided little incentive to seek part-time rather than full-time work. But in 1973 a new tax system was introduced, raising the threshold but abolishing the 2/9ths of earnings previously allowed: this provided a financial incentive to married women to work part-time, earning less than the tax threshold to avoid paying income tax.

The Reports of the House of Lords Select Committee on the European Communities (1982a) (1985) contain some interesting evidence on the effects of taxation and of national insurance contributions on the supply of female, part-time labour. For example, the evidence of the National Federation of Self-Employed and Small Businesses in House of Lords (1982) is cited in Chapter 7. More recently, the evidence of Symons and Walker (1986) suggested that tax allowances exert an important influence on the supply of part-time labour from wives. They show that if all wives were allocated the same income tax personal allowance, irrespective of whether or not they went out to work, which could be transferred to their husbands, then some 20 per cent of females working for less than seventeen hours a week would leave the labour force. In addition, their statistical evidence implies that there would be a fall of a further 17 per cent in the total hours worked by female part-timers.[6]

These results follow from simulations of a complex model of the supply of labour, based on cross-section data from the Family Expenditure Survey in 1981. Their work is continuing and has been updated to 1985, with modified results. Alternative assumptions can easily produce different conclusions, but it is clear from their research that the supply of part-time labour is affected by personal tax allowances.

An important change in national insurance contributions came in 1975 when flat-rate contributions were abolished and contributions were related to earnings, with no contribution payable if earnings were below £11 per week. It is not suggested that these tax and national insurance thresholds were introduced in order to encourage the supply of part-time labour: any such effect was an accidental by-product of policy. Moreover such effects were not responsible for the tremendous increase in the employment of part-time workers in the 1950s and 1960s which were related to the demand for labour. The most that can be claimed is that in the late 1970s and 1980s, the tax and national insurance thresholds may have helped to maintain the supply of married, female, part-time workers. The substitution of part-time adult, female workers for full-time young labour could have contributed to the increase in youth unemployment, although it is difficult to measure its precise importance, Hart and Trinder (1986). Nevertheless, these indirect effects have probably been more important than the direct effects of disincentives to the supply of young labour arising from income tax and national insurance contributions.

CONCLUSION

Between 1952 and 1981 youth unemployment increased by some 470,000, according to Wells,[7] but the population aged 15–19 increased by 1.4 million. The increased supply of young labour over the years was so great that it must have had an important depressing effect on the market for young labour.[8] The job prospects of young people were further reduced by the strong upward trend in the participation of married women in the labour force, mainly as part-time workers. Competition from this source has been particularly strong in the distributive and service industries which have traditionally been major employers of young people.

The youngsters who have suffered most from these adverse trends in the youth labour market are the unskilled, untrained, bottom 50 per cent of the school-leavers. Moreover, they have not been helped by the traditional neglect of vocational training in Britain.

The system of taxes and benefits also contributed to the rise of youth unemployment. It is very difficult to measure their effects but the evidence suggests that they have induced some voluntary youth unemployment, though the amount is probably small. Taxes have had an indirect effect on youth unemployment by maintaining, and possibly increasing, the employment of those married women part-time workers who pay neither income tax nor national insurance contributions because their earnings are below the thresholds. A discussion of the measures which might neutralise these effects of taxes and benefits is reserved for Chapter 9, which also considers appropriate policies on education and training which might reduce youth unemployment.

5

THE DEMAND FOR YOUNG LABOUR

INTRODUCTION

The economists who believe that an insufficiency of aggregate demand has made a major contribution to our present mass unemployment acknowledge the importance of the effects of world recession but argue that this has been exacerbated by domestic monetary and fiscal policies, especially since 1979, to produce record levels of unemployment in general and of youth unemployment in particular. Several quantitative assessments of the effects of demand deficiency have been made using macroeconometric models of the United Kingdom economy[1] and the smaller disequilibrium models of the market for young labour estimated by Rice (1986) and by Junankar and Neale (1985) described in Chapter 3.

But expanding aggregate demand is likely to increase imports and exchange rate depreciation is unlikely to solve the problems created by an excessive propensity to import; the relevant price elasticities are small and, moreover, exchange depreciation might stimulate demands for wage increases. In the absence of some form of incomes policy, demand expansion might generate increases in prices and wages rather than in output and employment. It is extremely difficult to enforce an incomes policy. One major difficulty takes the prisoner's dilemma form; each trade union is unable to rely on other unions' compliance with the policy and is therefore tempted to evade it by seeking special deals. Thus the failure to implement an appropriate incomes policy, and a poor competitive performance in world markets, are inextricably linked to the demand deficiency explanation of the return of mass unemployment.

Neo-classical economists do not accept the demand deficiency explanation, even with these qualifications. They claim that it is only to be expected that simulations of Keynesian macroeconometric models show that demand deficiency is a major cause of unemployment; the simulations reveal more about the behaviour of the models than about the economy. They emphasise the importance of reducing real wages (or at least their rate of increase), and the effects of the substitution of capital for labour. Other economists, sympathetic to the structuralist explanations of unemployment, might emphasise the importance of two-sector models, one sector with excess demand for labour (the 'South') and the second with excess supply (the 'North'). They claim that increasing

Table 5.1. *Young labour as a percentage of labour force in key industrial sectors*
1951–81

	Males				Females			
	1951	1961	1971	1981	1951	1961	1971	1981
Manufacturing	6.2	7.5	6.8	6.4	18.6	16.7	12.3	10.1
Construction	8.7	9.7	7.6	8.9	–	–	–	–
Distribution	5.3	8.9	8.4	9.6	19.2	16.4	11.4	12.1
Services	10.6	6.9	6.0	6.8	9.5	9.6	6.9	5.8

Sources: Census of Population and table 4.3 e.g. Manufacturing, males, 1951; 348/(5740–95) = 0.062.
The long-term changes in the age, sex and industrial composition of labour 1951–81 are shown
in more detail in Appendix 5. To allow for the raising of school leaving age to 16 years, we may
define 'young' as the age group 16–19 years and exclude the 15 year olds in 1951, 1961 and 1971,
in calculating the percentage of the labour force which is young.

aggregate demand would merely increase wages and prices in the first
sector without increasing employment and output very much in the
second. Hence, our high levels of unemployment are attributable to structural imbalances rather than to a deficiency in aggregate demand.

Thus the demand deficiency explanation of unemployment is very
controversial and there is such a large literature on the subject that
it is impracticable to appraise it here.[2] However, many economists,
including the present author, believe that unemployment is so high that
supply-side measures alone are unlikely to reduce it to an acceptable
level; demand-side policies should also be used. The risk of wage inflation
can be minimised by concentrating the demand expansion on the long-
term unemployed in our inner cities, and this will be discussed in Chapter
9. Meanwhile, the present chapter deals with the effects of decreases
in the *relative* demand for young labour (that is, relative to adults and
other inputs) on youth unemployment. It reviews the main determinants
of the relative demand for young labour, other than relative wages which
are considered separately in Chapters 3 and 6.

INDUSTRIES AND THE DEMAND FOR YOUNG LABOUR

In 1971 the largest concentrations of young male employees were in
construction, distribution and miscellaneous services.[3] For young females
aged 15–19 years, the key industries were clothing and footwear, distribution, and insurance, banking and finance. Changes in these few industrial
sectors therefore have important effects on the demand for young labour.

Table 5.1 shows that the percentage of young males in manufacturing
and in construction in 1981 did not differ much from that in 1951, but
it increased in distribution and decreased in services. The percentage

of young females in each of the manufacturing, distribution and service industries fell considerably between 1951 and 1981. In 1981 these sectors employed 77 per cent of young working females and, together with construction, employed 81 per cent of young working males. Thus they are extremely important sources of the demand for young labour.

The decline in total male employment in manufacturing from 5.74 million in 1951 to 4.4 million in 1981 was remarkable enough, but the decline in total female employment in manufacturing from 2.6 million to 1.8 million was an even greater percentage fall; over 30 per cent compared with a 23 per cent fall for males. The explanations which have been advanced for the decline of manufacturing employment include lack of competitiveness, world economic depression, technical progress, substitution of capital for labour, rise of new industrialised countries and so on. They are sufficient to explain the long-term decrease in the employment of young males in manufacturing because their percentage fall 1951–81 of about 19 per cent was less than that of total male employment in manufacturing. But the fall in the employment of young females in the sector was over 61 per cent and requires further explanation. Part of this fall was due to the increased participation of young females in further education.[4] But part was also due to the substitution of adult, female, part-time workers for young, female, full-time workers.[5]

In the sectors of expanding employment, distribution and services, the shares of young females also decreased sharply, as can be seen in table 5.1. Young males increased their share of employment in distribution but decreased it in services. As shown by table 4.3 total male employment in distribution increased by relatively little, from 1.52 million in 1951 to 1.54 million in 1981. In services it increased from 2.7 million to 3.0 million 1951–81. But the really big increases in these sectors were in the employment of adult females; in distribution their numbers increased by 58.4 per cent while in services the increase was a staggering 77.8 per cent 1951–81.[6] Once again, much of these increases related to part-timers and hence the increase in numbers employed in these sectors was considerably greater than the increase in the aggregate volume of female employment measured by labour hours.

The remaining key industrial sector, construction, is important for young males. Total male employment in this sector increased from 1.3 million in 1951 to 1.5 million in 1981. Since the share of this accruing to young males was much the same over the period, they do not appear to have suffered any comparative disadvantage.

Major analyses of the prospects for employment in each United Kingdom industrial sector have been prepared by the Institute for Employment Research at the University of Warwick (1985) and by Rajan and Pearson (eds.) (1986) at the University of Sussex. The demand for labour in a particular industry partly depends on its output and this is reflected in the Warwick employment projections based on macro-economic models, including a dynamic version of the Cambridge Growth Project. The Institute of Employment Research (1985) forecasts employment changes 1984–90 of −529,000 in manufacturing, +3,000 in construction and +820,000 in professional and miscellaneous services. Employment in distribution is expected to change by very little but the increase in part-time employment in this sector is expected to continue so that by 1990 there will be over one million part-time jobs in the distributive trades.

Rajan and Pearson (1986) did not use any economic model to compile their forecasts of employment changes 1985–90, but asked over 3,000 large and small employers for their views on the numbers they are likely to employ in 1990. This method produced an estimated reduction in manufacturing employment of 466,000 1985–90, which is consistent with the Warwick projection. A continued decline of manufacturing employment implies that the required increased demand for young labour is unlikely to come from manufacturing industry.

The common view is that, as the result of technological progress, the demand of manufacturing industry for unskilled labour will continue to decline, although the demand for skilled labour to operate and repair the new computerised equipment will increase. Hence the job prospects for young people in manufacturing depend on the extent to which they are trained in the necessary skills. If there is a substantial improvement in the skills of the young labour force, it might be possible for youngsters to work for British firms manufacturing the new equipment which could be substituted for imported machinery. Unfortunately, past experience has shown that new advanced machines tend to be imported, so that the new manufacturing jobs generated by the increased demand for such equipment might go abroad.[7]

Rajan and Pearson (1986) suggest that employment in construction will fall by 93,000 1985–90, although this fall will be offset to some extent by an increase of 43,000 in self-employment (the celebrated 'lump'). This forecast does not augur well for young labour, especially those under twenty years; they do not usually have the skills or experience to become self-employed.[8] The Warwick forecast of an increase of only 3,000 employees in construction 1984–90 is equally unpromising for young labour. It would appear that the best chance of increasing the demand for young labour in the construction industry lies with a substantial increase in output.

Significant increases in youth employment are likely to be restricted to the service trades, including distribution. In the case of retail distribution, the broad conclusion of appraisals of employment prospects by

Brodie (1985), NEDO (1985), and Trinder (1986) is that the increase
in the number of part-time workers in retail distribution is likely to continue, and the number of full-time workers is likely to decrease. If young
people at the beginning of their careers require full-time jobs, rather
than part-time work, their employment prospects in distribution are not
very promising.

Attitudes will also need to change if the demand for young labour
is to be increased. The small-scale fieldwork reported in Trinder (1986)
suggests that some employers still believe that young people have lower
marginal productivity than other employees. A larger survey of 701
employers conducted for the Manpower Services Commission (1978)
found that, compared with older recruits, young people are less willing
to work, have lower levels of numeracy and training in the basic '3Rs',
are more untidy and careless in appearance, less able to communicate
verbally and less stable. This survey was undertaken before the development of the Youth Training Scheme. It is to be hoped that the training
and work experience provided for young people under this scheme is
raising the quality of their work and increasing employers' demand for
young labour. The decline in young peoples' grasp of the basic '3Rs'
was also mentioned by one employer in the case studies of Trinder (1986).
This employer, a large retailing organisation, had been testing young
applicants' skills in basic literacy and numeracy for many years and
was disturbed at the falling standards of their young applicants.[9] The
schools were blamed for this deterioration in quality. The possibility
that part of the lower quality of young labour, and its higher unemployment rate, is attributable to inappropriate education raises many important issues which are considered in Chapter 9. Meanwhile, let us turn
to the next possible cause of the fall in demand for young labour, namely
employment protection legislation.

EMPLOYMENT PROTECTION LEGISLATION

A series of employment laws enacted since 1970 may have hindered
the recruitment of young labour, particularly by firms which do not
have the managerial resources to cope with this legislation. The Employment Protection Acts tend to arouse most of the adverse comments from
employers. Among other things, these acts provide employees with the
right to claim for unfair dismissal, which seems to be regarded as the
most irksome of the provisions. If an employer wants to hire more labour
he can avoid such restrictions by engaging part-time employees; if they
work for less than sixteen hours a week they are usually excluded from
such employee rights. This solution is particularly attractive to those
firms wishing to retain their traditional informal methods of appraising

heir workers and obviously reduces the employment prospects of youngsters seeking full-time jobs. Thus there are good *a priori* reasons for sup-
posing that the Employment Protection Acts have reduced employment
in general and youth employment in particular; employers become reluc-
ant to hire young people, who are inevitably new or recent entrants
into the labour market with largely unknown qualities, if they cannot
readily dismiss unsatisfactory recruits. This line of reasoning is familiar
enough, but the evidence from surveys of employers, which is all that
is available, suggests that the effects of unfair dismissal law on recruitment
in general is so small that any important effect on the hiring of young
labour is most unlikely.

Daniel and Stilgoe (1978) surveyed 301 manufacturing establishments
to ascertain employers' views on the Employment Protection Act. The
unfair dismissals provisions received most criticism, but the survey did
not find that recruitment was being discouraged as a result. Only seven
respondents (2.3 per cent) suggested that their recruitment policies were
being affected by this legislation, which is so small that the true population percentage could be almost zero. A sub-sample of 36 plants, experi-
encing an upswing following decreases in product demand and in manpower, yielded more significant results; twelve of the sub-sample reported
that their recruitment policies were being affected. However, more
detailed interviews revealed that these effects took the form of managers
being more careful about hiring employees rather than refusing to hire
at all; employment legislation affects the *quality* rather than the *quantity*
of recruitment.

One qualification is that small firms were under-represented in their
sample; indeed those with less than 50 employees were excluded completely. This shortcoming was remedied by Clifton and Tatton-Brown
(1979) who sampled 301 firms with less than 50 employees and obtained
similar results to those of Daniel and Stilgoe (1978). More recent research
on the effects of unfair dismissal law on employment practice has been
carried out by Evans, Goodman and Hargreaves (1985). They undertook
interview-case studies of 81 companies (52 with less than 50 employees)
in manufacturing, construction and service industries in Birmingham,
Reading and Sheffield. Their results confirm the earlier findings summarised above. Only six firms (8 per cent) were reluctant to recruit additional
labour because of possible unfair dismissal claims in the future. However,
there was evidence of the increasing use of temporary contract or casual
workers to meet economic uncertainty.

These studies show that the unfair dismissals provisions did not have
a major direct effect on the level of employment. Perhaps this was because
firms had become used to these provisions, which were originally introduced in the 1971 Industrial Relations Act, long before Employment

Protection Acts. Nevertheless, the Government decided to relax some of the provisions of employment protection legislation in their Employment Acts of 1980 and 1982. For example, small firms with less than twenty employees were exempted from the unfair dismissal provisions the qualifying period for employees was increased to two years, and the period of exempted 'fixed term' contracts was reduced from two years to one year. Moreover, in his 1985 Budget Speech, the Chancellor of the Exchequer announced that legislation would be introduced to extend the relaxation of unfair dismissal procedures from small firms to all employers. This became part of the Government's programme to increase employment by removing the unnecessary restrictions or entrepreneurs, especially in small firms, which were thought to be inhibiting the creation of jobs. Two White Papers, *Lifting the Burden* (1985) and *Building Businesses – Not Barriers* (1986) specify detailed lists of the restrictions to be removed.

DEMAND FOR SUBSTITUTES

Two possible substitutes for young labour are considered here and the importance of each varies across industries. The first, adult female part time workers, is particularly important in distribution and services. The second, capital equipment, is probably more important in manufacturing but partly because it is a substitute for both young and adult labour its effects on the demand for young labour are difficult to measure.

The extent of the general substitution of adult female part-time workers for young labour in the long term was described in Chapter 4. A more detailed analysis for the distributive trades is provided by Trinder (1986 and is summarised in Chapter 7. This substitution results from both the supply-side effects discussed in Chapter 4 and the demand-side effects considered here. Unfortunately, it is difficult to assess the influence of relative wage rates on employers' decisions to employ adult female part timers instead of young full-time workers because the most important source of wages data, the New Earnings Survey, excludes part-timers with earnings below the NIC threshold, the very people likely to be hired instead of youngsters.

Firms do not have to pay employers' national insurance contributions if the earnings of part-timers are below the NIC threshold, of £39 a week in 1987. Thus it is cheaper to hire two part-timers at, say, £38.90 a week than one young full-time worker at £77.80 a week. In 1980 some 40 per cent of female part-time workers were below the national insurance threshold (Martin and Roberts (1984)). The higher non-wage costs of full-time labour are more likely to deter small firms than large firm from recruiting young full-time labour. Nevertheless, all firms have an incentive to minimise non-wage labour costs and the lower costs of part-time workers can be expected to produce a substitution of part-time workers for those young full-time workers with whom they compete. This demand-side effect reinforces those noted in the previous sections in this chapter, namely the employers' belief that adult, female labour is of higher quality than that of youngsters, and the fact that part-time workers working less than sixteen hours a week are usually outside the scope of employment protection legislation.

Output is produced by labour, capital equipment, raw materials, and other factors of production such as energy. To what extent are these inputs substitutable for each other? In particular, to what extent has capital equipment been substituted for labour, especially young labour, thereby decreasing the demand for labour at any given output? To provide rigorous answers to these extremely difficult questions, an appropriate theoretical model has to be formulated and then estimated. But modelling the way capital equipment affects the demand for labour is controversial.[10] Furthermore, some of the theoretical models cannot be estimated because the data required are not available; for example, vintage production functions, with embodied technical progress, require data on the ages of capital equipment, and possibly of labour, to make some allowance for the heterogeneity of inputs used to produce a particular output.[11]

Hence many econometric analyses of the demand for labour ignore capital.[12] Of the seven econometric studies of the demand for young labour discussed in Chapter 3, only that by Abowd et al. (1981) included a measure of capital, although Hutchinson et al. (1984) used time trends to reflect the influence of changing capital equipment and technology. The coefficients of the linear and quadratic trends were significantly different from zero and usually indicated a positive effect on the demand for young labour. But this result might well indicate that the upward trend in numbers unemployed is due to many forces besides capital which are changing over time. Abowd et al. (1981) found no systematic time trend, possibly because they included capital, but suggested that capital and women are substitutes in production. However, their results were based on an estimated translog cost function using factor shares in total costs which might vary over time as the result of changes in supply in addition to changes in demand. As noted in Chapter 3, there is an identification problem which remains to be solved.

Meanwhile, more limited answers to the questions on factor substitution are available. First, surveys such as those summarised in Chapter 7 on the distributive trades show that capital has been substituted for labour. Secondly, for manufacturing, some preliminary econometric results indicate that in the aggregate capital and labour are substitutes.[13]

However, no separate estimates for youth employment are given. Thirdly, the national insurance contributions of employers and the tax allowances on capital expenditure have substantially increased the ratio of labour cost to the cost of capital and such changes in relative factor prices are likely to have led to a substitution of capital for labour, especially at the margin when a firm is considering whether to change to more capital-intensive methods of production.[14] These tax incentives supplement the effect of changes in technology. Fourthly, the common view is that automation has led to unemployment as capital is substituted for labour and, as indicated by Prais (1986), there is probably considerable truth in this view.[15] Finally, the evidence summarised by Hamermesh (1985, p. 73), on the substitution of capital and labour in other countries, suggests that capital and skilled labour are complements, but capital and unskilled labour are substitutes; 'tax credits for investment in new capital equipment (which lower the cost of capital) will produce decreases in the relative employment of young (presumably unskilled) workers ...' For all these reasons, the conclusion reached here is that capital equipment has been substituted for young labour.

CONCLUSIONS

Youth unemployment is so closely related to aggregate unemployment that any attempt to assess the extent to which it is caused by demand-side factors inevitably leads to the central macroeconomic controversy on demand deficiency. The literature on this topic is so vast that it would need at least a whole book, rather than a single chapter, to cover it. Hence, the present chapter had the more modest task of analysing the relative demand for young labour, beginning with the changes in industrial structure likely to affect the demand for young people relative to adults. The service trades, including retail distribution, are a traditional source of jobs for young people. Since the future employment growth of services seems to be more assured than that of manufacturing, the changing industrial composition of the demand for labour might well favour young labour. However, the service sectors also have a growing number of part-time jobs, rather than full-time jobs, which might not be suitable for youngsters entering the labour market. The employment prospects in manufacturing are poor for unskilled labour, but young people trained in the skills required in modern industry should be able to obtain jobs.

Young people are particularly vulnerable to the application of the LIFO (last-in-first-out) principle, so often used by firms and unions to determine redundancies. In view of this, it might be thought that youngsters are the very people who need the safeguards against dismissal provided by the Employment Protection legislation. But a common view is that young people seeking employment are hindered by such legislation; employers have become reluctant to hire them because they cannot readily be dismissed if they prove to be unsatisfactory. The survey evidence does not support this view, but the Government has relaxed various provisions of this legislation in the belief that the job prospects of young people were being reduced. If this belief is correct, the demand of employers for youngsters should be increased.

There are cost disadvantages of employing youngsters which stem from the tax and national insurance system. The non-wage costs of part-time labour are lower and hence employers have an incentive to hire part-timers rather than youngsters seeking full-time jobs.

The limited evidence available suggests that capital equipment has been substituted for young labour, particularly in manufacturing. Capital and labour generally appear to be substitutes. Where there is complementarity, it is between capital equipment and skilled labour, but until they learn the necessary skills, young people may be regarded as substitutes rather than as complements to capital equipment. Hence the increasing technological nature of industry probably tends to reduce the demand for unskilled youngsters.

6

YOUTH UNEMPLOYMENT IN
FRANCE AND GERMANY

INTRODUCTION

The tremendous increase in youth unemployment in the United Kingdom after 1973 was matched by that in France. Table 6.1 shows that in France the unemployment percentage for young males aged 15–19 years increased from about 5 per cent to 22 per cent 1974–82, compared with an increase in the United Kingdom from some 5 per cent to 27 per cent. However, there were important differences between the increases for young females in the two countries; in France from 10 per cent to 44 per cent, compared with an increase from about 4 per cent to 25 per cent in the United Kindom.[1] Thus, the rate for young females in France was even higher than in Britain.

In contrast, the increase in West Germany was from about 2 per cent to about 6 per cent for young males, and from about 5 per cent to about 10 per cent for young females. Lest these figures for 15–19 year olds be regarded as atypical, possibly as the result of the German apprenticeship system, it must be emphasised that the increase for 20–24 year olds in Germany was similar to that for their 15–19 year olds. Historically the 1982 unemployment rates were very high for Germany, but they

Table 6.1. *Unemployment rates in France, West Germany and the United Kingdom 1974–82, per cent*

	1974			1982		
	France	Germany	UK	France	Germany	UK
Males						
Under 20 years	5	2	5	22	6	27
20–24 yrs	3	2	2	13	6	14
25–54 yrs	1	1	1	4	3	5
Females						
Under 20 years	10	5	4	44	10	25
20–24 yrs	5	4	2	20	9	14
25–54 yrs	3	3	1	6	6	5

Source: 1974–82 OECD (1984) *Youth Employment in France*, Figures 1 and 2, pages 26–27.

Table 6.2. *Youth unemployment rates in France, West Germany and the United Kingdom 1982–5, per cent*

	1982	1983	1984	1985
France	19.0	19.7	24.4	25.6
Germany	9.5	10.7	9.9	9.5
United Kingdom	23.1	23.2	21.8	21.7

Source: OECD (1986) *Employment Outlook*, September, table 10, p. 31. 'Youth' refers to males and females under 25 years.

were very small compared with those in France and the United Kingdom.[2]

Table 6.2 shows that the unemployment rates for males and females under 25 years increased in France between 1982 and 1985. In West Germany this unemployment rate increased between 1982 and 1983 and then returned to its 1982 level by 1985. In the United Kingdom there was a slight decrease in this rate between 1982 and 1985. By 1984 the youth unemployment rate in France became even larger than that in Britain. Youth unemployment remains a serious problem in France and the United Kingdom and even in Germany it is high by their standards.

In previous chapters it has been argued that the upward trend in youth unemployment in the United Kingdom was due both to supply-side forces (such as demographic trends, income tax thresholds and national insurance contributions, inadequate training) and to demand-side forces (such as the substitution of adult married women for youngsters, and the substitution of capital for labour in general). The present chapter compares particular influences on the supply and demand for young labour in the three countries in order to see whether the explanations advanced for increased youth unemployment in the United Kingdom hold for the other two countries. The supply-side forces are considered first in sections on demographic trends, education and training, and taxes and benefits. These are followed by sections on substitutes for young labour, industrial composition and, finally, relative wages.

DEMOGRAPHIC TRENDS

Table 6.3 shows that, compared with a rise of 11 per cent in the United Kingdom, in France there was an increase of only 0.2 per cent in the population of 15–24 year olds 1971–81.[3] Yet there was a substantial rise in youth unemployment in France. There were also substantial increases in the proportions of young people in full-time education over this period which would have counteracted the small increase in the

Table 6.3. *Numbers and activity rates of young people in France, West Germany and the United Kingdom, 1971–81*

Population		France	Germany	UK
15–24 years (millions)	1971	8.48	8.10	8.12
	1981	8.50	10.13	9.01
% increase		0.2	25.0	11.0
Activity rates %				
15–19 year olds				
Males	1971	35.2	64.0	58.5[a]
	1982	22.4	44.5	56.8[a]
Females	1971	24.8	61.2	50.3[a]
	1982	16.7	37.0	51.4[a]

Source: OECD (1984) *Youth Employment in France*, tables 1 and 3, pp. 22–23.
[a] Great Britain only.

potential labour supply.[4] For France, the increase in youth unemployment cannot be attributed, even in part, to demographic trends.

Of the seven countries compared by OECD (1984), Germany had the largest percentage increase in the number of 15–24 year olds. There was an increase in unemployment among this group in Germany, but it was still well below the unemployment rates in France and the United Kingdom (Wagner (1986)). A reduction in activity rates for young males (but not for females) aged 20–24 years over this period no doubt helped to slow down the increase in unemployment (Wagner (1986) and table 6.3). Part of this reduction in male activity rates is attributable to greater participation in further education, but this was not the only force limiting the increase in unemployment; the subsidised repatriation of foreign workers also reduced the labour supply. Nevertheless, such factors were small relatively to the increase in the numbers of young people, and the fact remains that Germany managed to restrict youth unemployment to modest levels, by today's standards, in spite of most unfavourable demographic trends. It seems likely that the German training system which removed 15–19 year olds from the labour market, improved their job chances when they reached the 20–24 year age group; their specific skills, and their general vocational training, were still wanted by the labour market although technological progress was reducing the demand for unskilled labour. There are also other important differences between these countries which bear on youth unemployment.

EDUCATION AND TRAINING

The German training system is very advanced compared with that in the United Kingdom. Under the German dual system, a school-leaver combines practical training in a firm with theoretical training on day release at a vocational school, in an apprenticeship programme of between two and three and a half years. This leads to the practical and theoretical examinations which he or she is required to pass in order to become a skilled worker. The Federal Vocational Training Act 1969 specifies training requirements for some 450 occupations. The costs of the vocational schools are borne by the federal states, and the costs of within-firm training are borne by the employers. Over 1.7 million German youngsters were in the dual system in 1984 and the yearly intake was equivalent to two thirds of 16 year olds. There is still an excess demand of German youngsters for training places of some 200,000. Moreover, the breadth and depth of the German apprenticeship programme is much greater than in the United Kingdom, which augurs well for Germany's competitive advantage in the years to come (Wagner (1986)). The higher skill content of the young German labour force must have helped to reduce the impact of technological progress, with its increasingly complicated capital equipment, on the demand for labour; the demand for unskilled workers was reduced, but there is still scope for skilled young workers to operate, maintain and repair modern equipment.

The successful German youth training programme is founded upon their excellent schools system. While the educational performance of the more able English pupils compares well with that of the more able German pupils, the performance of English pupils in the lower half of the ability range lags behind their German counterparts by two to three years (Prais and Wagner (1985)). In these circumstances it is not surprising that youth unemployment in the United Kingdom is particularly serious for the low achievers at school; they do not yet reach the standards required to receive the training in modern skills which could help them to withstand the competition from their counterparts abroad.

Like Britain, France has belatedly recognised the importance of providing its young people with skills to enable them to cope with rapid changes in technology. In 1971 the French Government started to strengthen technical education and in 1977 it established the *lycées d'enseignement professionel* to provide skilled craft training leading to the CAP (*Certificat d'aptitude professionelle*) and to the BEP (*Brévet d'études professionelles*). It also formed the *lycées techniques* to train technicians, leading to the BTS (*Brévet du technicien supérieur*). In 1982 the Government declared that by 1985 no young person between sixteen and eighteen years should be without a vocational qualification. Moreover, the vocational training in schools should be supplemented by work experience in a firm. A series of measures, culminating in the training law of 1984, and the socially useful work programme of 1984 (*Travaux d'utilité collective*), should reduce youth unemployment in France but it is too early to assess the impact of these measures. Some 600,000 young people per annum will be covered by the various schemes and they could make an important contribution to the international competitiveness of French industry (Marsden (1986)). The fact that youth unemployment in France is still high in spite of improved training provisions shows that there are other causes of youth unemployment besides lack of training.

TAXES AND BENEFITS

Although unemployment and social security benefits are alleged to create voluntary unemployment, it has not proved possible to establish a strong link between the high youth unemployment in the United Kingdom and social security benefits. There is anecdotal evidence that unemployed youngsters are drawing social security benefits, to which they are at present entitled even if they refuse to join a YTS programme, while working illegally in bars, restaurants and in other casual jobs. But there is no hard evidence that such abuses are widespread.

In France, social security benefits for the young unemployed are more limited (Marsden (1986)). In order to qualify for the standard unemployment benefit (*allocation de base*), young unemployed people in France have to have made contributions for at least 91 days over the previous year. Nor are they entitled to this benefit if they left their previous job voluntarily. These provisions prevent many young job-seekers from receiving any benefits. School-leavers are entitled to a special benefit (*allocation forfaitaire*) while seeking their first job, but it is lower than the standard rate. The conclusion drawn by Marsden is that alternative incomes for the young unemployed in France are low, often zero, and that these youngsters live at home and depend on their parents. Yet in spite of the less generous benefits available to the young unemployed in France, the rate of youth unemployment is just as high as in the United Kingdom. The scope for decreasing youth unemployment by decreasing their benefits seems very limited.

In Germany, there is no incentive for young people to become unemployed voluntarily (Wagner (1986)). They do not usually fulfil the requirements for unemployment benefit, including the need to have held a job for at least one year during the past three years before becoming unemployed. In 1984 only 38,500 young people under twenty years, equivalent to 21 per cent of the young unemployed, received such benefits. The relatively low level of youth unemployment in Germany is consistent with the hypothesis that unemployment and social security benefits in the United Kingdom induce voluntary unemployment among young people. But it seems likely that the German educational and training systems provide occupational pathways for their young people which remove any incentive to drop out and become voluntarily unemployed. Young Germans, including the lower achievers at school, see the prospect of an apprenticeship leading to a proper job and this carrot is far more important to them than is the stick of zero benefits in their decision to reject voluntary unemployment.

SUBSTITUTES FOR YOUNG LABOUR

The German and French tax and social security systems do not provide the same incentives for the substitution of married women part-time workers for full-time young labour as do the British systems.

France and Germany do not have the British system of tax thresholds. In France the incomes of husband, wife and children are aggregated and then divided by a number determined by one for each adult, a half for each child (except the third which counts as one). Tax is levied on the quotient income. In Germany, a married couple can choose between separate taxation on each spouse, or taxation on the simple average of their incomes. Normally the latter is more advantageous. In neither country is there any tax incentive for a housewife to take a part-time job in order to earn a tax-free income up to a threshold determined by a personal allowance.

The German tax system, however, does levy only a 10 per cent rate on the earnings of part-time workers earning less than 42 DM a day, or not more than 120 DM a week if twenty hours are worked. But this incentive to part-time work is very weak because the incomes involved are very low by German standards. To use the illustration of Wagner (1986), a German saleswoman could work only ten hours a week at trade union rates before becoming liable to pay tax and social insurance. Her counterpart in the United Kingdom could work over eighteen hours a week before reaching the NIC threshold. Hence it is unlikely that there has been any significant substitution of adult married women for young labour in Germany as a result of the tax and social insurance system. This is borne out by the lower proportion of female part-time workers in Germany and, of course, by the lower rate of youth unemployment.

France also has a smaller proportion of female part-time workers than the United Kingdom which is the result expected from the French quotient system for determining income tax. But the proportion of adult women working full-time is considerably higher in France than in either Germany or the United Kingdom, which may be one reason why the unemployment rate of young females under nineteen years reached 43.4 per cent in France in 1981.[5] The higher proportion of adult females working full-time in France is no doubt linked to the fact that the cost of child care (for children under three years) may be deducted from income for tax purposes. This exceptional tax provision has presumably helped the growth of the numerous day nurseries in France which enable mothers to undertake full-time work.

The system of social security contributions in France is complex. There are different contributions for family allowances, old age, industrial accidents, life assurance, and unemployment, with some paid solely by employers, some solely by employees, and others paid by both employer and employee. Moreover, there are different systems (*régimes*) for the self-employed, those employed in agriculture and for other employees.[6] But there is no lower earnings limit such as occurs in the British social security system and hence there is no incentive for French housewives to obtain part-time work and earn up to that limit. Nor is there any incentive for a French employer to hire two part-time workers instead of one full-time worker; since part-time workers would have earnings below the critical level (*plafond*), he would have to pay health insurance contributions of 13.45 per cent on each part-timer's wage.[7]

There is a lower earnings limit for the payment of social insurance contributions in West Germany. But as pointed out by Schoer (1986) this limit was equivalent in 1983 to about 14 per cent of the average wage in Germany, compared with the much higher limit in Great Britain which was then 23 per cent of the average wage. He also associates this higher limit with the greater proportion of part-time workers in Great Britain. As a result of the different contribution thresholds, some 30 per cent of British workers are not protected by the social insurance system, compared with 11 per cent in West Germany.

Thus the French and German tax systems, unlike the British, do not encourage the employment of adult part-time workers instead of young full-time workers. However, the French tax concessions on child care payments encourage more mothers to undertake full-time work, and may explain why the female youth unemployment rate in France is so high.

INDUSTRIAL COMPOSITION

We have seen that the reduction in demand for young males in British manufacturing may be viewed as part of the reduced demand for labour in general in this sector. But the reduction in the number of young females in manufacturing of 61 per cent over the same period was much greater than that for all females. Even in the expanding sectors of distribution and services the share of young females in employment decreased sharply, contrasting with the increase in the employment of adult females by nearly 60 per cent in distribution and by 78 per cent in services between 1951 and 1981.

In France the changes in the industrial composition are somewhat different (Marsden (1986)). Agriculture is far more important than in the United Kingdom, and even in 1983 it had over 9 per cent of the male, and some 7.5 per cent of the female, employed population. This compares with under 3 per cent and under 1 per cent for the United Kingdom in 1981. Thus the decline in employment in French agriculture marks a major shift in the industrial composition of labour; in 1968 some 16 per cent of the French male working population, and 15 per cent of females, were employed in agriculture. The decreased employment opportunities in agriculture were extremely severe for young people under 25 years. For example, between 1975 and 1983, employment of young males fell by nearly 32 per cent and of young females by 37.6 per cent. The decline in agricultural employment is likely to continue.

After increasing in the 1950s and 1960s, employment in manufacturing fell between 1975 and 1983. The percentage falls in employment of young people in manufacturing were even greater than those for workers over 24 years. In France, as in the United Kingdom, there seems more chance of expanding employment in the service trades than in manufacturing. Male and female employment increased in distribution, transport and telecommunications, market services, banking and finance, and non-market services over the period 1975–83. However, employment of young people *decreased* in these trades over the same period. This reversal of fortunes for young females was even greater than that for young males. There appears to be a substantial substitution of older people for younger people in the expanding industries in France.

Germany also experienced a massive reduction in its agricultural labour force, which declined from 4.1 million in 1957 to 1.5 million in 1983; the share of 16–19 year olds in this employment fell from 9.7 per cent to 6.0 per cent (Wagner (1986)). Employment in energy, manufacturing and construction increased by about 700,000 over this period. But between 1970 and 1983, 2.5 million jobs disappeared in manufacturing and mining, while employment in services increased by 1.9 million. Over the longer period 1953–83, employment in transport and distribution declined slightly from 4.7 million to 4.6 million. Unfortunately, it proved impossible to separate the transport figures from those for distribution in 1957 so the changing age composition in the distributive trades cannot be ascertained. However, for the service sector as a whole, Wagner (1986, tables 3.5b and c) was able to show that female part-time employment increased from 117,000 in 1957 to 898,000 in 1982, even though part-time is defined as less than 23 hours a week in 1957 compared with a limit of twenty hours in 1982. With these definitions, female part-time workers formed only 3 per cent of all service employees in 1957 compared with 10 per cent in 1982, and 6 per cent of female employees in services in 1957 compared with 20 per cent in 1982. While the proportion of female part-time employees in Germany is much lower than in the United Kingdom, it is increasing in the very sector which has expanding employment.

RELATIVE WAGES

The hypothesis that the demand for young labour in the United Kingdom has fallen because the wages of young people relative to adults has been too high was investigated in Chapter 3. It was seen that six econometric studies confirmed this hypothesis but had used data which were unrepresentative of young people's wages. One econometric study based on alternative data rejected this hypothesis. The evidence is therefore inconclusive. Is there any evidence from France or Germany to support the belief that the demand for young labour would increase if their relative rates of pay were lower?

France has a system of minimum wages and young people are normally entitled to receive an adult wage on reaching eighteen years. Yet Martin (1983) found no statistical evidence to support the hypothesis that minimum wages affect youth unemployment in France. In addition, Marsden (1985) notes that since the early 1970s there has been no increase in the relative pay of young people, but the rate of youth unemployment has increased sharply. Indeed, the high levels of youth unemployment in the early 1970s may have halted the increases in relative pay which had been occurring in the 1960s. The same could be true for Britain. There does not appear to be any evidence from France which can be used to justify the belief that the abolition of Wages Council minimum wage rates for youngsters in the United Kingdom will have much effect on youth unemployment.

Further supporting evidence for this view may be found in Marsden and Ryan (1986) who show that the average relative pay of young people in the United Kingdom in 1972 was less than in Belgium, France, West Germany, Italy and the Netherlands. In addition, Marsden (1985) shows that for young male manual and non-manual workers the average relative pay in the United Kingdom in 1979 was less than that in France and West Germany. However, in both sources the dividing line between young and adult is taken as 21 years and it is possible that a lower age might be more appropriate. After all, a typical young German 19–20 year old has completed his apprenticeship, has been examined, and found to be skilled. Because such qualified young people are entitled to receive full pay rates they will raise the average pay of under 21 year olds in West Germany.

If 'young' is defined as eighteen years, then Kane (1986) has shown that in the United Kingdom their pay, relative to that of adults over 21 years, was 34.9 per cent for males and 48.3 per cent for females in 1984. Corresponding figures for 1979 were 39.7 per cent and 56.0 per cent, and he argued that the decline in the relative pay of young people, when youth unemployment was increasing rapidly, did not support the Government's claim that reductions in relative pay would reduce youth unemployment. But the counter-argument has been noted already; the decline in relative pay of young people 1979–84 was a consequence of the increase in youth employment, following from the weaker market for their labour. To reach a firm conclusion on the link between relative pay and unemployment, we need an identified simultaneous equations model containing both supply and demand equations for young labour.

The trouble is that the time series data needed to estimate such a model are either too short or unrepresentative of important markets for young labour. Hence we have to rely on less rigorous analysis, including the cross-country comparisons of the ratio of young people's wages to those of adults. However, such comparisons are superior to econometric analysis in at least one respect; they can be made for more detailed types of young labour to ensure that like is compared with like. Thus, when contrasting the levels of youth unemployment in Germany and the United Kingdom, it is important to study the relative pay of apprentices, rather than young labour as a whole, in each country. Jones (1985) provided such a study and showed that the relative pay of apprentices in Germany was much lower than in the United Kingdom. In Germany, this ratio increased from about 30 per cent of the skilled adult rate in the first year of apprenticeship to about 40 per cent in the final year. In the United Kingdom in the same industries, this ratio increased from about 50 per cent in the first year to some 90 per cent in the final year. Over the whole term of the apprenticeship the British youngster receives about 75 per cent of the adult wage rate whereas the German youngster receives 30–35 per cent.

The relatively low pay of German apprentices is confirmed by Wagner, who shows that in 1984, for example, the average pay of an apprentice electrician was 20 per cent of that of the newly qualified electrician. For car mechanics this relativity was 24 per cent. In 1980 these relativities were 26 per cent for sales personnel, 24 per cent for office personnel, and only 19 per cent for hairdressers. These percentages are lower than those in the examples used by Jones (1985, 1986).

In these circumstances it is hardly surprising that German firms are prepared to take so many apprentices while British firms are willing to take so few. Thus the effect of high relative wages of apprentices in the United Kingdom is that fewer young people receive proper training for a job as a skilled worker, and the increasing proportion of untrained, unqualified and unskilled workers are finding it more difficult to obtain jobs as the demand for skilled labour increases relatively to that for unskilled.

CONCLUSION

France and the United Kingdom had higher levels of, and greater increases in, youth unemployment than West Germany over the years since 1974. The increase in the unemployment of young females was exceptionally severe in France. West Germany had the most unfavourable demographic trends with their numbers of young people aged 15–24 years increasing by 25 per cent 1971–81 compared with 0.3 per cent for France. Yet West Germany managed to achieve the lowest rate of youth unemployment. There are several reasons for this.

The activity rates of young people in Germany fell more quickly than those in Britain partly because of the greater increase in post-compulsory education. But activity rates of young people in France were even lower than those in Germany. In fact, it is likely that part of the increased participation in further education in France may be explained by the desire of young people (particularly girls) to seek refuge from the unfavourable market for young labour. Thus the increased participation in further education in West Germany is not the major reason for its more successful record in providing jobs for young people.

A major reason for this is its education and training system which produces more skilled labour, as shown by Marsden, Trinder and Wagner (1986). France is improving the training of its young people but is still lagging behind Germany. The United Kingdom is also changing its training system, but probably lags behind France. This is certainly true for the building trades, as shown by Prais and Steedman (1986).

The fact that unemployed young people (under twenty years) in Germany do not usually receive unemployment benefits removes the incentive for voluntary unemployment. This might explain part of its lower youth unemployment rate compared with the United Kingdom, where a small part of youth unemployment is likely to be voluntary, as noted in Chapter 4. But such incentives cannot be all that powerful because the incomes of the young unemployed in France are very low, often zero, and yet youth unemployment is disturbingly high.

There are probably stronger indirect effects of the tax and social security system on youth unemployment through the replacement of youngsters by adult females in the labour market. In the United Kingdom, the income tax and social insurance thresholds encourage housewives to seek part-time employment and employers to provide it. Such tax threshold incentives do not exist in France or Germany and hence they have lower proportions of adult female part-time employed. However, France provides a unique tax concession to females by allowing them to deduct the cost of child care from their incomes for tax purposes. Hence, France has a larger proportion of adult females working full-time. It also has a much larger proportion of unemployed young females. It would appear that the tax and social insurance systems in France and Britain encourage the replacement of young labour by adult female labour although for different reasons.

The changing industrial structure also affects the employment prospects of young people. Agriculture is more important in France and Germany than in the United Kingdom and the decline in agriculture has considerably reduced the numbers of young agricultural workers in these countries. Britain has not experienced this particular problem. However, it has shared the experiences of France and Germany in the decreasing employment in manufacturing and mining. The service trades, including distribution, banking and finance, provide the best chances for increased employment. In Britain, however, these are the very industries where part-time jobs for adult females are increasing. In France, adult employment in these trades increased between 1975 and 1983, but the employment of youngsters *decreased*. The substitution of older for younger labour in the expanding industries appears to be even greater in France than in the United Kingdom.

The hypothesis that increases in youth unemployment have occurred because their wages have increased relatively to those of adults is common enough. There is conflicting econometric evidence and perhaps greater emphasis should be placed on the non-econometric results of Jones (1985, 1986). These reveal such high relative wages of United Kingdom apprentices, compared with those in Germany, that British employers become reluctant to train youngsters in the very skills required in modern labour markets.

7

THE CASE OF RETAIL DISTRIBUTION

INTRODUCTION

It has been argued earlier that the growth of female employment, particularly of part-time workers, and the upward trend in youth unemployment are linked; female part-time workers have replaced full-time young workers, partly as the result of income tax and national insurance contribution thresholds. What are the other forces leading to this change and how important are they compared with the fiscal causes? This question is difficult to answer, if only because part-time employment is far from homogeneous; there are many different kinds of part-time work and to make progress in assessing the relative importance of the different causes it is helpful to investigate a labour market which is less heterogeneous than the whole of British industry. Retail distribution is a convenient industry to choose for more detailed investigation. It is traditionally a major employer of young people, especially females, and has experienced a most rapid increase in the proportion of female part-time workers; for shop assistants, this proportion increased from 10.2 per cent in 1951 to 51.5 per cent in 1981 (see table 4.5). Moreover, the proportion of female part-time workers in retail distribution has continued to increase since 1981.[1] There have been several studies in recent years which relate directly to this growth, such as those by Robinson and Wallace (1974) (1978) (1984), Craig and Wilkinson (1985), NEDO (1985), and Trinder (1985) (1986). Let us consider each in turn.

ROBINSON AND WALLACE (1974) (1978) (1984)

The above authors recognise that the growth of female part-time employment has been influenced by employment protection legislation and by national insurance thresholds, but they place more emphasis on changes in selling methods involved with the rise of self-service stores, the combination of six-day trading with a five-day full-time working week, the extension of opening hours and late night shopping, and the increasing use of Saturday-only staff. This emphasis on changes in selling methods as a cause of increasing part-time employment was based on the authors' earlier survey (1974) of nine department stores, two multiple organisations, and two cooperative societies for 1971/2. But the important change in flat-rate national insurance contributions, with none levied on earnings below the threshold, took place in 1975, after the survey by Robinson and Wallace (1974). Furthermore, their sample of eleven retailers was not claimed to be representative of the retailing industry, or of any particular part of it, and certainly cannot be regarded as representative of the small retailers who seem to have the strongest objection to the costs of being involved with national insurance and PAYE.

The findings of Robinson and Wallace (1984) were based on a sample of 65 establishments, including 21 hospitals and 30 establishments in manufacturing, but only one in retailing. The latter had 545 employees of whom 457 were female; including 259 female part-timers or some 56.7 per cent of female staff which compares well with the 55 per cent national average in 1981. Although we cannot generalise from this one retailing establishment, it is interesting to note the institutional reasons given for the growth of its part-time employment. The desire of an employer to meet fluctuations of trade throughout the day with hiring part-time staff to cover peak hours is obvious enough. So are the advantages of hiring workers for only four hours a day; they do not have to be paid for the lunch hour if they work from, say 8.30 to 12.30, or 1.30 to 5.30. But the use of part-time workers to meet fluctuations in demand is not a new practice in British industry, as indicated by the examples of agriculture and the docks. Moreover, the problem of the peak has always existed in retailing, and it is just as much a problem in other countries. Yet, the proportion of part-timers increased five-fold in British retailing 1951–81 and it is much higher in Britain than in most other countries in the OECD. Part of the explanation must be United Kingdom-specific. One possible explanation is the low hourly wage rates of part-time workers, to which we now turn.

Robinson and Wallace (1978) show that the gross median hourly rates of pay of adult, female, full-time workers in retail distribution in 1975 exceeded those of part-time workers. The excesses ranged from 1.8 per cent for sales assistants up to 9.4 per cent for Retail Drapery, Outfitting and Footwear Wages Council rates. In addition, they noted (page 472, paragraph 13) that adult, married, female, part-time workers sometimes received less than the Wages Council rates per hour due to 'miscalculations'. In their words (page 474, paragraph 165), '... it is difficult to envisage that lower hourly rates paid to part-timers will not depress the demand for full-timers'.

The rates of pay studied are gross of tax and national insurance. But the supply of labour depends on net or take-home pay and the demand for labour depends on the cost to the employer, which is gross pay plus employers' national insurance contributions. The gap between the demand price and supply price of labour is important. Trinder (1986) used Wages Council rates for full-time and part-time shop assistants to show that this gap for full-time workers reached 34 per cent of the supply price, in October 1985. For part-time workers with earnings below the national insurance and income tax thresholds, the gap between demand and supply prices is zero. If the supply prices of full-time and part-time labour were compared, by using net instead of gross hourly wage rates, the differentials observed by Robinson and Wallace (1978) would be reduced substantially.

While it is illegal to pay less than the minimum wage rates stipulated by the Wages Councils, it is fairly common for actual market wage rates to be above these minimum rates. It seems likely that employers in areas where they have to pay above the minimum rate for full-time workers, will be able to squeeze the economic rents obtained by part-timers from paying zero taxes and insurance contributions, by not paying them more than the Wages Council rates. Market wage rates for full-timers are raised by income tax and employees' insurance contributions, because these reduce the supply curve of labour. They are lowered by employers' insurance contributions, which reduce the demand curve for labour. The outcome is that the gross hourly earnings of full-timers exceed those of part-timers, and that employers substitute part-time for full-time workers. Young people entering the labour market naturally want full-time jobs and the national insurance and income tax thresholds put them at a disadvantage in the competition with married women, part-time workers for jobs in the distributive trades.

CRAIG AND WILKINSON (1985)

Craig and Wilkinson show that the hourly earnings of female, part-time, shop assistants were below those of female, full-time, shop assistants from 1972 to 1982. There was no tendency for the ratio of part-time to full-time hourly earnings to fall over this period, yet the upward trend in the number of part-time workers continued. This might seem odd, until it is remembered that such ratios, based on the New Earnings Survey of gross hourly earnings, do not capture the effects of taxes and insurance contributions on the supply and demand prices of labour, which are so important for part-time employment. Another major limitation is that the data exclude many part-time workers whose earnings are below the national insurance thresholds.

The time series of earnings of full-time workers might be a more reliable guide to the effects of relative wages on relative employment. Craig and Wilkinson use the median earnings of the occupational category, selling, a somewhat broader group than shop assistants, to show that there was no tendency for the pay of young people to increase relatively to that of adults during 1974–82. Yet the unemployment of young people, relative to that of adults, increased over this period.

Craig and Wilkinson undertook their own survey of wages and employment. They selected a sample of 71 independent retailers in four retail trades (twenty grocers, 21 in confectionery, tobacco and newspapers, fourteen in hardware, and sixteen in menswear). In addition they included eighteen national multiple companies. The aim was to investigate the relationship, if any, between Wages Council minimum wage rates, inflation and jobs of both adults and young people.

They noted the tendency to employ married women as part-time workers in order to avoid paying national insurance contributions, but they did not consider the effects on youth employment. They were primarily concerned with the effects of lower wages of *all* retailing workers on employment in these trades. Only 9 per cent of their respondents cited increased wages as the main reason for reductions in employment, 33 per cent cited decline in trade/squeezed margins/insufficient trade/increased costs, while 48 per cent reported no change or even an expansion of business. The authors found that changes in wage levels played a relatively unimportant role in determining the quantity and quality of labour which retailers wished to employ. The level of economic activity was found to be the main determinant of employment: retailers would increase employment only if trade increased. Wages Council minimum wage rates do not have an important independent effect on employment, according to Craig and Wilkinson.

The retailers' responses to questions on the type of employees they would prefer to recruit are also interesting. Of the 71 independent retailers, no less than 35 would prefer to hire adult, female, part-time workers, and fifteen would prefer to hire adult women on a part-time or full-time basis. Only eight would prefer to recruit youngsters. The general preference of retailers for adult female labour is based on their belief that youngsters are inferior workers, but some respondents (one national food chain and six independents) mentioned the high relative pay of youngsters as one reason for their decision to reduce the proportion of youngsters they recruited. In 1986 the Government excluded young people from the protection of the Wages Councils and so this reason will no longer hold if the labour market is free. The quality problem is more difficult to overcome.

NATIONAL ECONOMIC DEVELOPMENT OFFICE (1985)

In March 1985 the Distributive Trades EDC issued a report on Employment Perspectives and the Distributive Trades which concluded that these trades are unlikely to generate a significant increase in employment.

Indeed, there is likely to be a long-term downward trend in employment as the result of the substitution of capital for labour. This substitution is due to technological progress and to the diversion of trade from labour-intensive to capital-intensive stores. The outlook for youngsters in this sector, which has traditionally been a major employer of young people, seems bleak.

It was recognised that the number of part-time jobs might increase, but this increase would be insufficient to outweigh the decrease in the amount of labour required as more capital-intensive methods increased labour productivity. The effect of relative wages on relative employment found by Wells (1983) was regarded as largely unproven, which is consistent with the findings of Chapter 3. However, the report accepted the argument in Craig and Wilkinson (1985) that the level of wages and employment in the retail trade largely depended on the overall level of demand in the economy. It did not consider the effects of income-tax thresholds and national insurance contributions on relative wages of young people and hence on their relative employment. Nor did it consider the effects of high first-year allowances against tax on the increased capital-intensity of selling.[2] Of course, the substitution of capital for labour is due in part to technological progress, but it is likely to have been accentuated by taxation policy, with subsidies to capital and taxes on labour. In the absence of changes in policy, to neutralise the bias in the national insurance system in favour of part-time employees, and to counteract the tax incentives to substitute capital for labour, the report's prediction of no significant increase in employment in distribution might well be justified.

The general thrust of this report is that the increased capital-intensity of distribution is due to irreversible technical changes which will persist in the future and which will reduce the numbers of workers in terms of full-time equivalents. Technological progress, with increasing self-service and changes in shopping methods, underlies the downward trend in manpower requirements of the distributive trades and there is little scope for more jobs for young people in these trades. However, this view is qualified by the work of Trinder (1986) which is considered in the next section.

TRINDER (1985) (1986)

Trinder (1985) shows the striking long-run changes in the age and sex composition of shop assistants; in 1921 in England and Wales some 48 per cent were male, but by 1951 this percentage had declined to 33 per cent and in Great Britain by 1981 it had fallen to only 16 per cent. Nowadays this occupation is predominantly female. In 1921 some

33 per cent of all shop assistants in England and Wales were young people (of both sexes) below the age of twenty years. By 1951 this percentage had fallen to 24 and by 1981 (for Great Britain) it was only 18 per cent. Young people formed a larger proportion of the population, and of the labour force, in 1921, so demographic changes were responsible for some of the decline in the proportion of retailing jobs for young people. Another part of this decline was due to more youngsters continuing their education. But a major part must have been due to the employment of adult married women instead of young shop assistants. Only 5 per cent of shop assistants in 1921 were married women aged 25 to 59 years. This increased to 22 per cent by 1951 and to 48 per cent by 1981.

This switch of retailing jobs from young women to older women 1951–81 is discussed in more detail by Trinder (1986). Emphasis is rightly placed on the growth in the number of part-time jobs for older married women for the reasons of taxation and national insurance mentioned earlier. But part of the explanation of the reduction in retailing employment (measured by full-time equivalents) was the Selective Employment Tax which was expressly designed by the Government to divert employment from retailing to manufacturing. This tax also provided an incentive to reduce hours of work because it was not paid on employees working for less than 21 hours. The abandonment of Resale Price Maintenance was another Government measure which encouraged retailers to reduce staff.

That technological progress has led to the substitution of capital for labour in retailing is also accepted. This takes the form of new products, transport development, new methods of handling goods, new packaging, new retail equipment, scanners for bar codes, computerised stock control and so on. Against this is the well-known tendency for consumers to increase their expenditure on services as their real incomes rise. They might seek more help at the checkout counters of self-service groceries, they might require someone to box their purchases and take them to the car, or even to deliver them to their homes! Consumers in future might be prepared to pay more for shop assistants who know something about the goods being sold. Which E-additives in our food are not allowed in other countries? Which is the appropriate adhesive for attaching plastic to metal? Will this fashionable bri-nylon swimming costume disintegrate in a chlorinated swimming-pool? Of course, shop assistants who could reduce the consumers' need to do their own research would have to be better educated and trained to provide such retailing services. The scope for ill-educated and for untrained staff is obviously very limited in an age of sophisticated products. But with better education and training, young people might find jobs once more in retailing.

The fieldwork reported in Trinder (1986) did not always confirm the view that national insurance thresholds encouraged employers to hire part-time rather than full-time labour. The personnel directors of the large retailers interviewed agreed that their part-time employees were often anxious to ensure that their hours of work were kept low enough to avoid paying employees' contributions and naturally their desires were met, as far as possible, by their employers. But even if the desire to avoid paying such contributions is stronger for employees than for large retailing employers, the fact remains that the latter also gain by avoiding a significant increase in their labour costs. The representatives of the smaller retailers were less inhibited and freely admitted that one reason for hiring part-time labour was to avoid paying employers' contributions. Furthermore, the fact that such employees did not pay income tax either reduced the costs of their employers who did not have to finance expensive PAYE administration.

The desire of married women, part-time workers to avoid paying tax and national insurance was clearly expressed by the National Federation of Self-Employed and Small Businesses Ltd, in its evidence to the House of Lords Select Committee on the European Communities (1982a). Mrs Pauline Yeardley, the secretary to its EEC Committee stated: 'I feel qualified to speak on this because, for twenty years, I have had three thousand ladies coming through, and working for me, and the first thing they say when they come in is that they do not want to earn above the limit that they start to pay for a pension or tax, because they have been instructed, most of them, by their husbands to make sure they do not earn above that rate.'

When part-time work reduces the taxes of both employee and employer, it is reasonable to suppose that they will act in accordance with their common interests and ensure that weekly hours are kept below the threshold levels. Hence, taxes and national insurance thresholds encourage part-time work and discourage full-time work.

CONCLUSION

There has been a major substitution of adult, married women, part-time workers for young full-time workers (especially young females) in retail distribution since 1951. Technological change, increased opening hours of shops, superior quality of adult, part-time shop assistants, and the need to meet peak demands, have contributed to the rise of the part-time labour force, but they do not explain why the proportion of part-time shop assistants in the United Kingdom is so much higher than in comparable industrial countries. Other countries have peak period trading, technological change, and so on, and there must be explanations specific to the United Kingdom for its greater substitution of part-time labour for full-time shop assistants. These United Kingdom-specific factors include the thresholds for paying national insurance contributions and income tax. In addition to the direct effects on the demand and supply of part-time labour, they also tend to reduce the market hourly wage rates of part-time labour. An employer can avoid paying national insurance contributions by hiring part-time workers, and also pay lower gross hourly wage rates to his part-time staff without making their net, take-home, hourly pay, which governs their labour supply, less than that of full-time workers. That is, part of the wedge between market gross and net wage rates is absorbed by employers, instead of the Government.

The employment of young full-time workers in retail distribution might be increased if the Government made the appropriate changes in its policies on national insurance contributions and income tax. Its existing Youth Training Scheme will do something to improve the quality of young labour and will increase their chances of obtaining a job in retailing. But more needs to be done, as explained in Chapter 9. Perhaps the biggest problem is to change the attitudes of employers, and of employees, to training. If more young people were employed and trained in off-peak periods, the need to employ part-time staff to meet peak trading hours would be reduced. But before British retailers could be persuaded to emulate German retailers' training programmes it might be necessary to bring the relative pay of apprentices nearer to that in Germany.

8

SPATIAL ASPECTS OF YOUTH UNEMPLOYMENT

INTRODUCTION

The between-countries comparisons in Chapter 6 suggested reasons for the different levels of, and increases in, youth unemployment in France, Germany and the United Kingdom. Further insights into the underlying causes of the rise of youth unemployment may be obtained from the spatial analyses within the United Kingdom alone, as shown in the present chapter. These are concerned with important aspects of youth unemployment, such as the problems of various disadvantaged groups, which are not revealed by the time-series analysis in earlier chapters. Unskilled and unqualified young people tend to experience extreme difficulties in obtaining stable jobs, especially if they are non-white. Such disadvantaged groups may not be able to compete for jobs in the kind of segmented labour market which exists in the United Kingdom, in contrast to the continuum of pure markets in the neo-classical economic model outlined in Chapter 1. Barriers between different labour markets are important and the two-sector model described in the structuralist approach is probably a closer approximation to reality, although there are obviously more than two sectors in practice.

A spatial analysis is very useful in the specification of segmented labour markets but it may not always be appropriate for assessing explanations of the rise in youth unemployment. For example, there is no spatial variation in unemployment benefits (at least in money terms), so there would be no point in trying to relate unemployment to benefits across different locations.[1] Again, youth unemployment tends to be high in locations where adult unemployment is also high, so a spatial analysis would not add anything on the effects of adult unemployment already noted in the time-series analysis in Chapter 2. However, in other instances spatial analyses are essential aids to our understanding of the causes of youth unemployment; lack of mobility and housing tenure are important examples. Furthermore, important data on qualifications, or on ethnic groups, are often more readily available for different locations than for different years and justify a spatial analysis even if there is no specific effect of location on youth unemployment.[2] Thus spatial aspects of youth unemployment merit discussion before the various policies to reduce it are considered in Chapter 9.

Table 8.1. *Unemployment rates in urban and rural areas, 1951–81 (indices, Great Britain = 100)*

Residents of	1951	1981
Inner cities	133	151
Outer cities	81	101
Free standing cities	95	115
Towns and rural areas	95	90

Source: Begg *et al.* (1986) in Hausner (1986), vol. 1, p. 20.

SPATIAL VARIATIONS IN UNEMPLOYMENT

The variation in unemployment rates across different geographical regions of the United Kingdom is large enough to suggest that there are two nations. The relatively prosperous one comprises the South East and East Anglia.[3] These two standard regions have lower unemployment rates than the others which, together with their higher *per capita* gross domestic products, permit us to regard them as the prosperous sector 1 in a two-sector model with the remainder of the country forming the relatively poor sector 2. Moreover, these regional disparities of unemployment are increasing over time (Armstrong and Taylor (1987)). However, there remain important disparities within regions and it certainly does not follow that all locations in sector 1 are more prosperous than all locations in sector 2. For example, the economic and social problems of Hackney (part of London and in sector 1) are more severe than those of Harrogate (in Yorkshire and in sector 2). Once again, the two-sector, or two-nation, classification is merely a simple approximation to the multi-sectored labour market.

The increasing spatial variation in unemployment rates is also seen from the Census of Population data on unemployment which may be classified by urban and rural areas as in table 8.1. The relative increase in unemployment in our inner and outer cities, and the relative decrease in unemployment in our smaller towns and rural areas, are sometimes associated with a long-term drift of industry from our large conurbations to greenfield sites.[4] This long-term spatial shift in sources of jobs is not revealed by the time-series analysis of Chapter 2 and yet is clearly relevant to economic policies aimed at improving the job prospects of youngsters in our inner cities.

Table 8.2 summarises the spatial variation in the unemployment rates of young people in 1981, using Census of Population estimates which differ from those used in the time series in Chapter 2. The final column

Table 8.2. *Unemployment rates of young people by location, Great Britain, 1981, per cent*

	Growth areas	Inner London	Greater London	Other conurbations	Great Britain
Males					
Age 16–19	14.1	25.2	19.2	24.4	18.6
Age 20–24	11.6	18.0	14.0	21.7	15.9
All ages	7.8	14.0	10.1	15.5	10.9
Females					
Age 16–19	12.7	19.9	14.9	21.9	16.7
Age 20–24	8.4	11.4	9.2	14.6	11.1
All ages	5.5	8.9	6.7	9.1	7.1

Source: Census of Population estimates derived by Buck and Gordon (1986), table 4.

shows that in the whole country the unemployment rates for 16–19 year olds in 1981 were some 8 or 9 percentage points above the rates for all ages. The unemployment rates for 20–24 year olds were below those for teenagers, but still well above those for all ages. In each case, male unemployment rates exceeded female unemployment rates.

The unemployment rates were highest in Inner London and in Other Conurbations. The highest rates were for teenage males in Inner London and in Other Conurbations (25.2 per cent and 24.4 per cent). The long-term rise of youth unemployment appears to be linked to the long-term rise in unemployment in our inner cities. This is not to say that the spatial classification as such has a significant statistical effect on relative youth unemployment, for the ratio of teenage unemployment rates to those of all ages is much the same (between 1.6 and 1.9 for males, and between 2.2 and 2.4 for females) in different locations. It simply means that just as youth and adult unemployment rates are correlated over time, so are they correlated across space. The causes of increased adult unemployment rates in our inner cities have also increased youth unemployment there. Just as some economists contend that the rise of unemployment over time is due to demand deficiency, so do some regional economists claim that inter-area differences in unemployment rates are attributable to differing pressures of demand, Cheshire (1979), Gordon (1985). But perhaps the most important contribution of the spatial analysis of unemployment is its emphasis on the personal characteristics of the unemployed, which can be measured across space, using the Census of Population, the Labour Force Survey and other survey data. To these we now turn.

PERSONAL CHARACTERISTICS OF UNEMPLOYED YOUNG PEOPLE

Using Census of Population and Labour Force data, Buck and Gordon (1986) compare the unemployment rates of the unskilled, the semi-skilled, the unqualified, and the non-white males and females in the different groups of locations used in table 8.2. The unemployment rates of these disadvantaged groups are well above the average unemployment rates in each group of locations. For example, the unemployment rate for non-white females was 8.4 per cent in growth areas in 1981, compared with an average rate of female unemployment of 5.5 per cent in growth areas. Using logit functions, the authors were able to estimate the contribution of each kind of disadvantage to the probability of being unemployed. For example, a youngster was three times more likely than an older worker to be unemployed, and an unqualified worker was three times more likely than a qualified worker to become unemployed. Hence a young, unqualified worker was nine times more likely than an older, qualified worker to be unemployed. Being under 25 years significantly increased the probability of being unemployed. Those of Afro-Carribean or of Asian ethnic origin were also more likely to be unemployed.

Similar logit functions were estimated by Lynch (1987) from a sample of young people in five Greater London boroughs. She also found that ethnic origin had a significant effect on the probability of a youngster being unemployed. However, having a part-time job whilst still at school reduced the chances of a youngster becoming unemployed. The latter result is consistent with the findings of Main and Raffe (1983) based on their sample of unqualified Scottish school-leavers. In addition they found that those youngsters who were allowed to sit 'O' level examinations had a better chance of getting a job than those who were not allowed to take the examinations. Local unemployment rates also had a significant influence on their job chances. These results could be explained by employers using evidence of part-time jobs whilst at school, or of actually taking (though not passing) examinations, as a screening device when there is an excess supply of young labour. That is, employers regard youngsters with these attributes as likely to be more reliable workers than those who did not even sit the school examinations or who did not take a part-time job whilst at school.

The importance of qualification in improving the job chances of young people in the studies of Buck and Gordon, and of Lynch, could also be attributed to employers' screening. But there are other explanations. Rightly or wrongly, those employers with businesses being radically changed by modern technology may feel that it is too risky to hire unqualified youngsters to be trained to use expensive equipment (and materials);

they may believe that youngsters who have shown little sign of learning at school are unlikely to learn complicated procedures at work. There is less scope nowadays for employing unqualified youngsters.

The unemployment problems of our inner cities occur partly because individuals who suffer labour market disadvantage inevitably tend to live where there is the largest stock of cheap housing. Their disadvantaged youngsters attend inner city schools which so far seem to have been unable to overcome the formidable problems of teaching enough of their pupils to reach satisfactory standards; the Inner London Education Authority, Newham and Haringey are three of the five English education authorities with the highest proportion, 20 per cent, of school-leavers achieving no grades at 'O' level or CSE examinations against a national average of 11 per cent (Buck *et al.* (1986)). This educational disadvantage tends to lead to subsequent disadvantage in the labour market.

Additional insight into the rise of youth unemployment is provided by a series of urban case studies relating to Chelmsford, Leicester, Liverpool, London, St Albans, Stafford and Sunderland, which are discussed in the next section.

URBAN CASE STUDIES OF YOUTH EMPLOYMENT

Leicester, St Albans and Sunderland

Ashton, Maguire and Garland (1982) report the replies to a questionnaire on youth employment obtained from 350 employers in the above towns. They find that there are several labour market segments, rather than a continuum, but consider that the dual labour market hypothesis[5] of Doeringer and Piore (1971) is too crude; they argue that it is inappropriate to divide the many segments into just two groups (or sectors in the two-sector model of Chapter 1) such as a primary sector (prime-age, white males with qualifications), and a secondary sector (teenagers, blacks, married women and others marginally committed to the labour force). Thus, while the two-sector model, with its emphasis on the importance of barriers between labour markets, is a step in the right direction away from the one-sector neo-classical or Keynesian models, it is still an over-simplification of the complex labour markets in the real world with their restricted entry points for young labour.

They agree that the criterion of an internal promotion system, which is a characteristic of the primary labour market in the theory of Doeringer and Piore, is useful. Unfortunately, Ashton *et al.* measured the importance of internal promotion by the number of firms using it as a proportion of the number of firms sampled, without weighting by employment. For example, 34 firms in their sample with over 1,000 employees, had internal promotion systems and were probably responsible for more employment than the aggregate of small firms without internal promotion systems.[6] Thus the importance of the primary labour market is underestimated.

The same problem arises throughout the report, which is based on classifying numbers of employers rather than the employment provided. Thus they found that 51 per cent of employers had unskilled, or semi-skilled jobs for which they would not hire young people, because the jobs involved shift-work or other physical and legal requirements which youngsters could not satisfy. These employers also cited youngsters' irresponsibility, and in some cases the 'dead end' nature of the jobs, as reasons why they would not recruit youngsters. While we do not know the proportion of employment provided by these 51 per cent of firms, the finding that there are so many entry barriers for young labour is instructive nevertheless.

The authors postulate that employers first choose between competing groups of labour, such as males or females, young or adult. They then choose from individuals who compete with each other within a group. Some jobs are sheltered in the sense that they are available only to youngsters, some are closed and available to adults only, and some are exposed to competition between youngsters and adults. This classification of labour market segments is helpful even though the numbers of firms providing each type of job are not weighted by employment.

Educational qualifications were more likely to be required by the larger firms; small firms placed little reliance on them if only because their worker-proprietors often had no educational qualifications themselves. In any case small firms were less likely to recruit youngsters because training was too expensive and because their smaller numbers of employees generated fewer vacancies. The authors also noted that there had been a substantial decrease in the entry of youngsters into the distributive trades, traditionally a major entry point for youngsters, especially females. This was associated with the increasing number of part-time workers in shops and with the reluctance of employers to consider youngsters for part-time work.

The importance of the spatial level of unemployment as a determinant of the job prospects of youngsters is indicated by the differences between depressed Sunderland and prosperous St Albans. In Sunderland a quarter of school-leavers became unemployed, only 23 per cent continued schooling beyond the age of sixteen (compared with 60 per cent in St Albans) and they had less than half the chance of St Albans' youngsters of entering the professional and managerial class. Disadvantage generates more disadvantage.

Leicester, St Albans, Stafford and Sunderland

Ashton and Maguire (1986) extended their spatial analysis of the previous sub-section by including another town, Stafford, by interviewing

450 young people aged 18–24 years in addition to interviewing 28 employing organisations, and by considering young adults rather than school-leavers. They confirmed their previous finding that the labour market is segmented with institutional barriers between markets (such as those stemming from training) being very important. They also emphasised the importance of location, rather than social class as a determinant of the kind of jobs taken by young adults; St Albans youngsters from the lower working class have a greater chance of entering white-collar work than youngsters from middle-class families in Sunderland.

Those barriers to entry based on legal requirements, custom and practice, (such as shift-work, using dangerous machinery or possessing a driving licence) are lowered to 18 to 24 year olds, simply because of their age. Against this, the 18 to 24 year olds are normally excluded from employers' training programmes. Employers prefer to recruit 16 to 17 year olds for training and there is little scope for training later on.

Attitudes to training were influenced by job prospects; there is less incentive to undertake training in Sunderland where job prospects are low. In any case completing apprenticeships or undergoing training provided no safeguard against redundancy, notably in skilled occupations in Leicester. Indeed, with the increasing use of computers in manufacturing, there was a reduction in the demand for traditional craft apprentices and an increased demand for those with keyboard skills. In the financial services sector the increasing use of computers had reduced the demand for routine clerks/typists. In motor repair, the increasing use of sealed components tends to reduce some of the traditional mechanical skills required. The authors found some shortages of skilled labour which arise because employers' cuts in training programmes did not replenish the stock of skills.

The young adults were also questioned about their experience at school. Most had had some lessons directly related to work. Many were aware that their schools provided work experience programmes, although more were aware of this in Sunderland (78 per cent of males, 80 per cent of females) than in Stafford (12 per cent of males, 23 per cent of females). The efforts of Sunderland's schools in providing work experience programmes are worth noting. Most young people began their job search while at school or at college and most were dependent on their careers advisers for their knowledge of the labour markets. More had held part-time jobs whilst at school in prosperous towns (80 per cent of those in St Albans) than in depressed towns (40 per cent in Sunderland), presumably because the chance of obtaining a part-time job is higher in areas of relatively low unemployment. According to the logit functions discussed earlier in this chapter, having a part-time job improves one's chances of obtaining employment after leaving school. This is yet another example of success breeding success.

Chelmsford, Liverpool and Walsall

Roberts, Dench and Richardson (1986) surveyed 308 firms and 854 youngsters aged 17–18 years in Chelmsford, Liverpool and Walsall 1984/5. In Chelmsford, 8 per cent of the youngsters in the sample were unemployed compared with 41 per cent in Liverpool and 28 per cent in Walsall. Overall there was a 7 per cent decline in employment 1980–4. Job losses were particularly severe in manufacturing. Small firms were more successful than large firms in preserving old jobs, and in generating new jobs. Once again, the analysis of job losses is conducted in terms of percentages of firms, without weighting by employment, thus making interpretation difficult. A possible explanation is that firms in manufacturing tend to be larger than those in non-manufacturing and, since the recession hit manufacturing more severely than non-manufacturing, large firms lost proportionately more employees than small firms in the sample as a whole. Whether small firms did better than large firms within the manufacturing stratum is another matter.

The most common explanation of the decline in employment found by the authors was new technology; the numbers of displaced production workers exceeded the number of new high-level staff needed to design, install, programme and manage the new systems. The demand for unqualified youngsters for unskilled jobs collapsed; 'the bottom, not the top, of the young market fell away'. Firms adjusting to reduced labour requirements by 'natural wastage', or minimum recruitment policies, reduced the opportunities for young people to enter the labour market. The lower wages of youngsters were outweighed by their high supervision and induction costs. Recruitment policies were also affected by adult female workers taking maternity leave instead of leaving the labour force.

The authors stressed the importance of educational qualifications. They found that employers were still keen to employ well-qualified youngsters, with good 'O' levels and especially those acquainted with keyboards and electronic information. There was no point in expecting youngsters without any 'O'levels to undertake the part-time study required to obtain technical qualifications. They suggested that a polarisation of the qualified and unqualified was occurring. Even in Liverpool, with a 41 per cent youth unemployment rate, only 8 to 10 per cent of Liverpool girls with 3 or more 'O' levels were unemployed. However, location is still of fundamental importance; jobs in Liverpool which required candidates with 'O' levels were filled in Chelmsford by youngsters with the lower CSE levels.

London

The special problems of London have been mentioned earlier in this chapter. In addition, the sample survey of school-leavers in London (Tower Hamlets, Bromley, Hammersmith, Hounslow and Lambeth) undertaken by Richardson (1983) and a series of case studies of unemployment in London (Brent, Ealing and Southwark) by Gordon (1985), and Buck *et al.* (1986) have yielded interesting results.

Richardson found a clear link between unemployment and personal characteristics such as race, educational achievement, and family background, and clear differences between unemployment rates of inner and outer borough residents, especially for girls. While girls in the outer boroughs search for jobs locally *and* in the centre, girls living in the inner city did not seek work in the outer areas, even though they faced keen competition for local jobs from working wives, who naturally preferred to take jobs near their homes. To combat this, Richardson suggests that reverse commuting from the inner to the outer areas should be subsidised, at least for those up to eighteen years of age, in order to improve the job prospects of unemployed youngsters residing in the inner city. This proposal is extended in the section on mobility in Chapter 9.

Gordon and Buck *et al.* note that London has not escaped the national decline in manufacturing employment. In fact the decline in the metropolis has been accentuated by the movement of manufacturing firms out of London. This counter-urbanisation tendency will be reinforced by the completion of the M25, an orbital motorway around London, as firms move out to obtain better facilities for transporting their products. However, labour has also moved out so that the unemployment rate in London itself does not fully reflect the decline in manufacturing employment. But such a solution is not usually available to teenagers; they are not owner occupiers with accommodation to sell in London to finance house purchase beyond the Green Belt, nor are they council tenants in London with a tenancy to exchange. Hence, the outward shift of employment opportunities from London must have reduced the job prospects of young Londoners. Against this, London has traditionally provided major entry points into the labour market in the form of a wide range of white-collar jobs and in the lower stratum of service employment. Both types of job are over-represented in Inner London and not only help young Londoners but also attract young workers from outside the region. The availability of private rented accommodation in Inner West London has assisted this in-migration and the resulting increase in labour supply has increased unemployment in areas such as Brent and Ealing.

As in other parts of the country, jobs in London are becoming increasingly biased towards the non-manual types which require some qualifications and skill. Thus the unskilled and unqualified find it more difficult to obtain employment. In fact, the problem of inner city unemployment is largely concentrated on such teenagers who suffer because of firms' minimum recruitment policies and because of competition from older, married women. To these drawbacks must be added the disadvantages of youngsters from the ethnic minorities; the very high unemployment rates among young blacks is the strongest single factor in the local variation of youth unemployment rates within London.

Thus London's problem of youth unemployment is associated with the personal characteristics of the unemployed such as lack of qualifications, inadequate post-school training, disadvantages of ethnic minorities, and so on. Outward migration, together with changes in commuting patterns, have absorbed part of the effects of the decline in employment opportunities, thereby reducing the increase in the unemployment rate. But such adjustments to changing labour market conditions are constrained, first by rent-controlled accommodation, by restricted local authority housing, and by high and rapidly increasing house prices in the private sector. Secondly, labour mobility is constrained by the high costs of commuting. Such constraints must be eased, if it is desired to use increased labour mobility in order to reduce youth unemployment in London.

CONCLUSION

The analysis of spatial variations provides valuable insights into the causes of the long-term rise in youth unemployment. In 1952, when the time series of Chapter 2 begin, there were no problems of unemployed young blacks in our inner cities. Nor did the young whites living there experience serious difficulties in obtaining jobs, in spite of having neither educational qualifications nor training. Long-term changes in the composition of the young labour force and in the skills required for new types of job, have contributed significantly to the rise in youth unemployment. Their effects are revealed in the spatial studies.

These highlight the importance of the personal characteristics of the young unemployed. However, they do not distinguish between demand-side and supply-side effects. For example, having a part-time job whilst still at school decreases the probability of a school-leaver's becoming unemployed. But is this the result of labour supply signalling a keenness to work, or is it the result of the demand for part-time labour being higher in areas of low unemployment? Perhaps both supply-side and demand-side influences operate, but for the purposes of economic policy it might be important to know which are dominant. If the root problem of unemployment in our inner cities is the lack of demand, then targeted increases in demand are likely to reduce inner city unemployment. But if the real problems are on the supply side, with the unskilled and the unqualified living in the inner cities because of cheap accommodation, then even targeted increases in demand will not improve their job chances very much. Instead, such demand increases are likely to lead to more suitable workers commuting from outside the city to take the jobs created by the demand increases. In such circumstances it would be preferable to devote the extra expenditure towards inner city schools and colleges, to improve the qualifications and skills of the young people living there.

The spatial studies also emphasise the importance of labour market segmentation. There are real barriers between different labour markets which unemployed young people are unlikely to surmount without assistance. Improved education and training can help them to enter those segments requiring qualifications and skills, but such help is of little use if the relevant jobs are no longer available in their localities. Geographical barriers have to be reduced by other policies, as indicated in Chapter 9 which discusses supply-side and demand-side policies for youth employment.

9

POLICIES FOR YOUTH EMPLOYMENT

INTRODUCTION

Appropriate policies are needed to reverse the long-term upward trend in youth unemployment. In one respect it will be easier for the Government to reduce youth unemployment in the future than it has been in the past; future demographic trends are more favourable in the sense that the number of young people entering the labour market will decline in the rest of the 1980s, and this should make for a reduction in youth unemployment. It will also reduce the costs of supply-side programmes for employment because there will be fewer young people to educate, train, counsel, and so on.

Supply-side policies are considered first. They involve education, training, spatial mobility, benefits, taxes, and other special measures to reduce youth unemployment. Secondly, there is a discussion of demand-side policies targeted on specific areas of high youth unemployment. A possible third category of policies dealing with wages is excluded, on the assumption that the relative wages of young people will be left to be freely determined by market forces and negotiations between employers and trade unions. Those responsible for such negotiations, who believe that the training of our future labour force is of fundamental importance, may be influenced by the German dual system and the low relative wage of German trainees reported in Chapter 6. Government policies on non-wage labour costs and benefits are included in the discussion of the supply and demand for labour.

EDUCATION

While the level of youth unemployment remains very high, it is also true that the vast majority of our young people manage to obtain jobs. We are concerned here with the less successful of our young people and do not deal with the broader, and most important, issues of general educational policy which affect all youngsters. There is evidence to support the view that the top of the upper tail of the distribution of ability of pupils in England compares favourably with that in Germany, a competitive industrialised country. But it is clear that the lower half in England is inferior to that in Germany; in mathematics our worst sixteen year olds are something like two years behind their counterparts in Germany.[1] The problems of the unemployed, unskilled young people start in the schools; too many school-leavers are regarded as unsuitable for the technical training required in modern industry.[2]

How can the educational standards of our lower achievers be raised? Clearly, it is advisable to choose policies to raise standards which command the support of the school teachers and to do this it is probably necessary to increase expenditure on education, if only to provide extra payments to those with high transfer earnings, such as teachers of mathematics, computing, and other technical subjects. But it may be possible to devise policies which would raise the standards of our lower achievers without great increases in expenditure. The following proposals suggest that some improvement could be obtained with modest increases in expenditure, although the results would be better if more resources were provided.

(a)   The syllabus in each core subject (but not the curriculum) could be narrowed by providing a basic, standardised course. This would be consistent with the Government's proposal to introduce a national curriculum. Standardisation with common textbooks (at least for each bottom band) in each school in an educational authority, or even region, would also simplify teaching and training. The larger print run of the chosen textbooks would also reduce costs. Each pupil (and each teacher) would know precisely what he or she is expected to know at each age and performance could be monitored. Such procedures would amount to following the example of Japan.

(b)   Another Japanese practice which merits the most sympathetic consideration is the provision of extensive extra tuition for those pupils who need it. Extra tuition outside normal school hours would involve additional payments to teachers. Perhaps British parents, unlike Japanese parents, would be unwilling to cover the costs, even if they were an allowable deduction for income tax purposes. If so, there would be a case for financing it out of general taxation. Extra public expenditure at an early stage in the lives of our low achievers might save expenditure at a later stage. Scarce resources of training schemes would not have to be used to teach youngsters what they should have learned at school. Moreover, if extra help at primary or secondary school improves the job prospects of the low achievers, there will be savings in terms of social security payments, not to mention reductions in alienation and crime, at a later stage.

(c)   In France and Germany, the lowest achievers at the end of a school year are required to repeat the year's work on the grounds that they will be unable to cope with higher grade work. Thus progression to more difficult topics is not automatic, as it is in Britain, and so the lowest achievers are less likely to find that nearly everything being taught is beyond their comprehension. Perhaps we should follow the example of France and Germany.[3] It would not involve much extra expenditure. There might be problems arising from increasing the dispersion of ages in a single class, but France and Germany seem to overcome them. So can we.

(d)   In addition to the core courses designed to help pupils to be literate and numerate, there should be more vocational education, increasing the existing Technical and Vocational Educational Initiative (TVEI) by about ten-fold. Only 2 or 3 per cent of our pupils benefit from TVEI compared with some 30 per cent in France, Germany and Japan.[4]

(e)   Providing such pupils are making satisfactory progress, they could be given the chance to obtain work experience for two or three weeks at local firms in their final year at school or even the year before that, as in Berlin. Some schools in Britain already operate such schemes, so this proposal amounts to extending existing best-practice to all schools. It goes without saying that the local firms used should be monitored to ensure that they do not exploit youngsters (for example, by using them as cheap labour). In addition to providing pupils with some insights into the world of employment, such schemes would enable employers and potential employees to assess each other.

(f)   We could add the subject 'Work Tuition' to the curriculum along the lines of the German *Arbeitslehre*. The syllabuses could vary between different regions as they do between the German *Länder*. In Berlin, for example, the syllabus includes basic instruction in typewriting, reading of technical drawings, consumer information, role of national production standards and many other useful topics.

All these possible policies are controversial from the educational point of view. Some teachers will support them and might even argue that such policies should not be confined to the lower achievers but should cover all pupils. Other teachers will oppose them arguing that they conflict with the currently conventional educational methods. From an economic point of view, the choice is clear enough. The United Kingdom is part of a Common Market which includes France and Germany and those of our young people who cannot match their French and German counterparts in basic learning will tend to become unemployed, as we buy more goods from France and Germany which are of better quality because they are produced by labour of higher quality. Hence, either

our lower achievers improve their standards or they will be unemployed
However, an improved educational standard is not a sufficient condition
for obtaining a job; it is merely one of the necessary requirements.

The Youth Training Scheme is a belated attempt to catch up with the
training programmes of our competitors abroad and should be given
every encouragement to improve and extend its training content. It i
now two years in duration but it must be given greater vocational training
content from the first year, if we are to keep our French, German and
Japanese competitors within range (Prais (1986)).

The Job Training Scheme (JTS), which started in April 1987, assist
young unemployed people over eighteen years of age to train with an
employer for a recognised qualification. The Non-Advanced Further
Education (NAFE) is another step in the direction of improving the
quality of young labour (Davis (1986)). In this initiative the Manpower
Services Commission will support non-advanced technical and vocation
al education geared more closely to the requirement of local labour mar
kets. Such initiatives help to reduce our lack of competitiveness and
our unemployment but they are still inadequate.

One criticism of the emphasis on training programmes as aids to reduc
ing youth unemployment is that the supporting technological arguments
usually relate to manufacturing industry, now responsible for less than
26 per cent of total employment.[5] Not all of the expanding service sector
are undergoing technological change as rapid as that in manufacturing
For example, in the case of retail distribution, it might be argued that
the requirement for a more skilled labour force is less urgent than in
manufacturing. Indeed, some British retailers with YTS trainees might
find it difficult to extend the training programme for shop assistant
to two years. Yet German retailers provide three years of training for
their apprentices, with the third year containing more general skills such
as book-keeping, stock-keeping and so on. The teaching of general skills
is important partly because it improves the flexibility of young labour
A young German completing an apprenticeship as a baker might decide
to take a job in a firm making kitchen units; his general training, and
parts of his specific training, make him a more efficient machine operato
than the corresponding untrained, unskilled British operative.

Of course the need for training is not confined to young people. In
fact, one of the really critical limitations on our competitiveness might
be that our typical foreman cannot match the German *Meister*, Prais
(1987). To remedy this, further training for adults is required. This argu
ment may be extended to include British managers, for we also lag behind

in management training. More highly skilled leadership would improve the performance of our young labour and the increased competitiveness would improve their chances of retaining employment. Furthermore, such an increased investment in human capital of all ages would make it more attractive for multinational enterprises to locate manufacturing plants in the United Kingdom, rather than elsewhere in the European Community. Multinational enterprises are footloose and the availability of a well-educated, skilled labour force is very important for them. The attraction of new factories to our more depressed regions can make a vital contribution to the reduction of the unemployment of young people and of adults.

Improved training is an important supply-side policy for reducing youth unemployment. In terms of the two-sector model outlined in Chapter 1, the critical dichotomy might be between the trained and untrained labour with the former obtaining core jobs and the latter spending their time moving in and out of employment and sometimes competing with part-time workers for peripheral jobs. Extensive training will open core jobs to more young people and remove barriers to employment. But training policies by themselves must not be oversold as a cure for unemployment; they must be accompanied by flexibility, including retraining as new skills replace obsolete skills. There is no point in waiting until an electrician in a shipyard is free to move an electric cable on the grounds that it is electricians' work and nobody else may move it (Colin Hughes, *The Times* 7 January, 1984), for without flexibility shipbuilding costs are too high and the lack of competitiveness results in unemployment. Traditional restrictive practices of labour can thwart training programmes and in industries such as shipbuilding have been just as important a cause of industrial decline as the lack of adequate supplies of labour skilled in modern techniques. Thus training is another necessary, but not a sufficient, condition for increasing youth employment.

Massive increases in vocational education, training and flexibility, are necessary to prevent a further erosion of our competitiveness. It is not only necessary to run faster in order to maintain our existing position among industrialised countries; it is also essential to invest in our human capital to withstand competition from the newly industrialised countries. As noted by Lecraw (1985 p. 402), 'Singapore is no longer a low-income, low-wage country, its GNP *per capita* exceeds that of Hong Kong, Israel, Ireland, Greece, Portugal and Spain ... so that Singapore's labour intensive exports have come under increasing competitive pressure ... In order to compete ... Singapore can either restrain wages or increase the human and physical capital intensity of its manufacturing sector. Singapore is now undertaking massive investment in human capital'.

We in the United Kingdom have to run faster in order to avoid lagging even further behind.

SPATIAL MOBILITY

According to Green *et al.* (1985), on which the discussion here is based, the dispersion of regional unemployment rates is now very large and it might be thought that there would be a tendency for the rate of increase in wages to be lower in the high unemployment areas than elsewhere as a move towards restoring equilibrium in local labour markets. But this is not the case. Pay settlements vary only slightly across regions and large regional disparities in unemployment persist. Wage adjustments cannot equate the supply and demand for labour in different regions, possibly as the result of national wage negotiations. Is there scope for quantity adjustments on the supply side to reduce the inequality of unemployment rates between regions? In particular, would the movement of young unemployed people from north to south (across a Severn–Lincolnshire line) to fill vacancies in the more prosperous regions reduce both the dispersion and the mean of regional unemployment rates? If so, should such mobility be encouraged? If it should, how can it be done?

Internal migration tends to fall in a recession and some economists argue that a reduction in unemployment is more likely to increase labour mobility than an increase in mobility is likely to reduce unemployment. In any case most internal movements of population are not related to employment and, moreover, much of the employment-related migration is undertaken by employed workers (especially by those changing their jobs within the same firm) rather than by the unemployed. It is easier for an employed person than for an unemployed person in one region to obtain a job in another region; employers prefer to recruit an employed rather than an unemployed person. Hence, the young unemployed in a depressed area who seek jobs elsewhere have to compete not only with the unemployed but also with the employed workers for vacant jobs in the more prosperous area. In the circumstances the unemployed youngsters might well believe it is preferable to stay put, and to rely on local knowledge and contacts to obtain a job, or even to work in the local black economy. Those who take the risk of leaving familiar surroundings in order to seek a job in another region are likely to be the more enterprising, and more skilled, young people. They are just the youngsters the depressed region cannot afford to lose if it is to attract the new industries it needs for revival. Thus it is not certain that labour mobility should be encouraged; it might reduce regional unemployment in the short run, but it might make for lower employment in the longer run.

However, it might not be necessary for the young unemployed to travel very far to obtain work. The movement of firms from the inner cities to surrounding rural communities in the same region means that vacancies can arise within commuting distance. Nearly 30 per cent of aggregate unemployment is in the six largest cities (London, Birmingham, Glasgow, Manchester, Liverpool and Newcastle) and it might not be necessary for the unemployed in the cities to move house in order to obtain jobs in surrounding satellite towns. The problem for the young unemployed in the cities is that the high commuting costs absorb much of the difference between their net wages and social security benefits. To counteract this, there is a case for helping them to meet the public transport costs of their journey to work. In London, for example, which has nearly 14 per cent of the nation's unemployed, there is a massive inflow of commuters (mainly office workers) each day from surrounding areas and it would not be expensive in real terms to subsidise the reverse commuting of unemployed Londoners to factory jobs in the outer metropolitan areas. Little or no congestion cost would arise. Indeed a flow of new passengers travelling against the major flows in the morning and evening might ease the financial problems of public transport.

A remaining barrier to the mobility of young labour is the lack of information. It is known that about one third of successful seekers of jobs obtain the information on vacancies from relatives or friends, compared with about 17 per cent obtaining the information from Job Centres. How can the young unemployed in our great cities obtain information about jobs twenty or so miles away which might not be listed in their local Job Centres and which are unlikely to be known to their personal contacts? One answer, along the lines proposed by Green *et al.* (1985), would be to extend the computerised bank of vacancies in Job Centres to cover all jobs (not merely those difficult to fill) and to make it compulsory for Job Centre managers to display them, preferably on a visual display unit. It is not difficult, in principle at least, to spread information about job vacancies in the age of the computer.

BENEFITS AND TAXES

The traditional view is that unemployment and social security benefits encourage young people to remain unemployed. Extensive econometric investigation of the relationship between benefits and unemployment has not been able to produce any reliable confirmation of this relationship (Micklewright (1986)) Nevertheless, the suspicion persists that such benefits do provide an incentive for unemployment, especially for *some* young people even if it is not true for the *average* young person whose reactions are measured in econometric analysis. It is true that most young unemployed people do not have the contributions record to obtain any unemployment benefit. It is also true that the supplementary benefit to which they are entitled may be reduced by 40 per cent for six weeks if they refuse a reasonable job. But the fact remains that there are unfilled vacancies in the Youth Training Scheme and that some young people are happy to work in the black economy, possibly also drawing benefits, and are not prepared to undertake training for a regular job. To counter this, the Government intends to provide a YTS place for every school-leaver under eighteen who is not taking a job and plans to withdraw benefits from youngsters who refuse either a reasonable job or a place on the YTS programme.[6]

In France, many young unemployed receive no benefit and depend on their parents (Marsden (1986)). In Germany, unemployed people have to have held an insured job for at least one of the preceding three years in order to qualify for unemployment benefit, which effectively rules out most young unemployed people; only 21 per cent of the unem-ployed below twenty years of age received benefits (Wagner (1986)). Thus, if the United Kingdom were to withdraw benefits from those 16–18 year olds who refuse a YTS place or a job, it would simply be following the example of France and Germany.

As explained in Chapter 4, income tax affects youth employment as a result of increasing the supply of substitute labour, in the form of married women part-time workers, rather than as a result of reducing the supply of labour from young people. The appropriate policy to reduce this discrimination in favour of part-timers with earnings below the level of the wife's earned income allowance, would be to introduce tax allow-ances transferable between spouses, coupled with the replacement of the married man's allowance by a single person's allowance. Everyone would receive the single person's allowance, irrespective of whether he or she were employed. Transferable allowances would be likely to reduce the number of wives in part-time jobs.

After his 1986 Budget the Chancellor of the Exchequer presented a Green paper (*Cmnd* 9756) on the *Reform of Personal Taxation*, in which the proposal for transferable allowances was discussed. Most of the argu-ments concern the equity of moving part of the tax burden from one-earner married couples to two-earner married couples. Here we are con-cerned with the effects on youth unemployment, which is a different matter. However, the Green Paper touched upon this point by casting doubt on the view that transferable allowances would reduce the number of married women in employment, citing the case of Denmark which has transferable allowances and the highest proportion of married women working of any country in the European Community. Against this is the argument that Denmark's highly progressive tax system provides additional incentives for part-time work. The House of Lords Select Committee on the European Community in its 1985 Report on *Income Taxation and Equal Treatment of Men and Women*, took the view that transferable allowances would reduce the number of married women in jobs. On balance, the evidence appears to suggest that transferable tax allowances would reduce the supply of married, female, part-time employees and hence would increase the job prospects for unemployed young people, especially girls.

Chapter 4 also noted the effects of employees' national insurance contributions on the supply of female part-time labour. The Green Paper reviews the arguments for integrating employees' national insurance contributions and income tax. There is a strong case for such integration.[7] With integration and transferable allowances, the current incentive for part-time employees to work sufficient hours to reach the lower earnings limit would be removed; most married households with husband and wife at work would in effect contribute to the national insurance fund, as well as to income tax receipts, from the very first hour of a wife's (or a husband's) part-time job. Hence the integration and transferable allowances are likely to reduce the supply of labour from married women. Since this is likely to improve the job prospects for the young unemployed, it merits support.

The existence of the same national insurance threshold for employers' contributions also increases the demand for part-timers, as explained in Chapter 5. To remove the incentive to hire two part-time workers, instead of one full-time young worker, a simple payroll tax could be levied on employers for each employee; a simple percentage of the employer's payroll at the end of the fiscal year involves one calculation instead of separate calculations and recordings for each employee each week.

Of course such a tax would do nothing to remove the incentive to hire part-time workers in order to avoid creating a PAYE system. Moreover, it would still be a tax on labour which encourages the substitution of capital for labour. Such substitution is accentuated by tax allowances on investment. When the whole of the expenditure on capital equipment can be offset against tax in the first year, as under the first-year allowances 1972–84, it must be expected that capital will be substituted for labour. These first-year allowances were reduced to 75 per cent in 1984, to 50 per cent in 1985, and were abolished after March 1986. Thus the Government has recognised the bias in favour of expenditure on capital rather than on labour and is reducing it. While it might be argued that in a closed economy in the long run such investment allowances do not create a bias in favour of capital, because capital itself is embodied labour, the fact remains that in the open economy of the United Kingdom, advanced capital equipment is often imported so that foreign embodied labour receives the benefit of our generous tax allowances on investment. If more capital intensive production is cheaper, as the result of technical progress, then it should lead to some substitution of capital for labour. But there is no point in accelerating such substitution by taxing labour and subsidising capital, if such a policy simply increases unemployment above the level resulting from technical progress.

SPECIAL MEASURES: SUPPLY SIDE

Most of the Government's special measures to reduce unemployment affect the demand side of the labour market, but some supply-side measures are considered here, particularly the job-start allowance and early retirement schemes.

The Government's job-start allowance scheme provides £20 per week for six months to those unemployed for more than a year who take a full-time job with gross earnings of less than £80 a week. This allowance is paid directly to the individual employee and although it is subject to income tax it does not affect the employees' or employers' national insurance contributions. Job-start allowances should reduce the supply price of the labour of the long-term unemployed and the £80 threshold makes the scheme particularly important for young people. After six months it is to be hoped that those drawing the job-start allowance will prove that they are worth a pay rise of £20 a week from their employers so that the supply and demand prices will converge. At the very least, those on the scheme will become used to going to work and this itself should help them to retain employment.

Early retirement schemes reduce the supply of labour. If young people are substituted for workers retiring early, then youth unemployment will be reduced. Although the number of men in the labour force over 60 years of age has declined, the activity rate among older workers remains higher in Britain than in France or Germany (White (1986)). In Britain the state pension age is 65 years for men and 60 years for women. In 1973 workers in Germany with an adequate contributions record were permitted to retire on full state pension at 63 years. Moreover, the long-term unemployed over 60 years old can also obtain full state pension.

In France the state pension age for any person was made 60 years from 1983. In 1982–83 solidarity contracts were introduced for the 55–9 year olds who were given financial support until the age of 60 years providing they were replaced by new workers, especially by the young unemployed. An approximation to such a policy in Britain is the Government's Job Release Scheme, introduced in 1977. This enabled people approaching the retirement age to retire early with financial support until reaching the state pension age, providing their employers replaced them with people registered as unemployed. However, the numbers involved on the Job Release Scheme[8] are small and no expansion of the Job Release Scheme is planned, possibly because of administrative costs. That is, the Government's view is that other schemes are more cost-effective. Nevertheless, at least in principle, an extension of such early retirement schemes could help to reduce youth unemployment.

THE DEMAND SIDE

The aim of the remainder of this chapter is to review various demand-side policies, acceptable to different schools of thought, which should reverse the upward trend in youth unemployment. The view of neo-classical economists that the unemployment of a particular kind of labour may be removed by decreasing its wage rate relatively to other wage rates has received support from Mrs Thatcher's second administration which abolished the minimum wage rates for young people formerly set by the Wages Councils. It also abolished the employers' national insurance surcharge, thereby reducing the cost of labour relatively to capital. Furthermore, it reduced the disincentives to recruit labour which it believed were created by some employment protection legislation. Apart from eliminating such harmful effects on the demand for young labour produced by such regulations and taxes, the Government seems to assume that there is little it can do to influence the demand for British labour, which depends primarily on market forces.

The alternative view that the Government, through its monetary and fiscal policies, has had a considerable influence on employment does not necessarily imply that the appropriate policy to reduce unemployment is to increase aggregate demand. Such an increase might generate increases in prices and wages, especially in the more prosperous sectors of the economy such as South East England, rather than increases in aggregate output. Moreover, imports might absorb much of the increase in aggregate demand. Thus there are real difficulties involved in expanding aggregate demand. Are there any demand-side policies which can be implemented while avoiding the problems created by wage–price spirals and by our high propensity to import?

Let us consider the policies proposed by the CBI (1985), by Layard, Metcalf and O'Brien (1986) and by Britton (1986a). Though these proposals were made to reduce aggregate unemployment, they are highly relevant to the reduction of youth unemployment. However, their chances of success would be increased considerably if the supply-side policies just discussed were implemented. Supply-side and demand-side form a convenient classification of policies but they are not independent. For

example, if British unemployed young people had more vocational training, so that they were more competitive at current wage rates with their
counterparts in other industrialised countries, there would be a greater
chance of fiscal expansion generating increases in domestic output and
employment rather than in imports.

Layard *et al.* propose to target the increased demand on the long-term
unemployed in our inner cities. The CBI proposals for increased public
expenditure are more general but are of the same type, whereas Britton's
proposal for increasing public sector employment is more specific.

Targeted increases in demand

The basic idea of these proposals is to focus the increase in demand
on the long-term unemployed in our inner cities, on the grounds that
their need is greatest and that their reemployment is unlikely to stimulate
wage inflation. It is also less expensive than general measures to increase
aggregate employment, such as tax cuts. Since nearly 39 per cent of
the 1.58 million long-term unemployed are below the age of 25 years,
these proposals are particularly important for decreasing youth unemployment.[9] The Government already intends to expand its Community
Programme to provide work for about 250,000 of the long-term unemployed so there is a good precedent for these proposals. Both the CBI
and Layard *et al.* envisage a substantial increase in the building programme. The latter's National Renovation Scheme is designed to repair
our decaying inner cities. Expenditure *now* on our decaying infrastructure
such as housing, schools, hospitals, roads and sewers will save far greater
expenditure on such infrastructure in the future; the underlying theory
is that a stitch in time saves nine and seems eminently reasonable.[10]
The total amount of extra Government expenditure proposed, after allowing for the reduced payment of unemployment benefits and increased
receipts from income tax and national insurance contributions, is of critical importance. Layard *et al.* estimate that their targeted demand expansion would increase the public sector borrowing requirement by about
£1 billion per annum for three years. However, this is a serious underesti-
mate, according to Lobban (1986). Before reaching a decision on the
various proposals it is essential to have firmer estimates of the costs
of financing them. But at least in principle it seems sensible to target
increases in demand on the long-term unemployed in the inner cities.

Layard *et al.* also suggest that more jobs for long-term unemployed
should be provided by the health and social services, which certainly
need more helping hands. But even if the finance were provided, and
even if the public sector trade unions agreed to work alongside such
recruits, there would still be the problem that the creation of jobs
in the health and social services would do very little to increase our

international competitiveness. The same criticism applies to the National Renovation Scheme and was clearly stated over fifty years ago by Professor T. E. Gregory in Addendum III to the Macmillan Committee Report.[11]

The third proposal of Layard *et al.* is to subsidise firms taking on long-term unemployed to the extent of £40 per week per person, providing the firms' non-subsidised employment does not fall. Once again, the merits of this kind of marginal employment subsidy have been discussed in detail long ago in the 1930s, in the Economists' Report to the Economic Advisory Council (1930). These economists (Henderson, Keynes, Pigou, Robbins and Stamp) doubted whether it was possible to determine the number of extra employees requiring the subsidy. They thought that profitable firms would complain that the subsidy would be a bounty to the inefficient firms and, furthermore, firms receiving the subsidies might undercut those not seeking wage subsidies.[12]

A more recent appraisal of marginal wage subsidies is provided by Rajan (1985), who surveyed employers' reactions to the subsidies they obtained under the Young Workers' Scheme. He also asked for their views on a wage subsidy proposed by Layard, similar to that in Layard *et al.* Rajan found that initially of every 100 jobs attracting the wage subsidy, 80 would have existed in any case (the deadweight loss), four were created by substitution for adult workers (the substitution effect) and only sixteen were new jobs (net incremental effect). In time the extra jobs would reach 20, or even 25 per cent. That is, at best, for every job created, three other jobs attract the marginal wage subsidy. Similar conclusions were reached on the Layard scheme and hence the forebodings in the Economists' Report (1930) seem justified; marginal wage subsidies are a very expensive method of reducing youth unemployment.

It would appear that the first two proposals in Layard *et al.* should be given priority over their third proposal for wage subsidies. There is a strong case for the Government to provide useful work for our long-term unemployed, possibly in some kind of National Renovation Scheme. It might be true that such schemes will do little to increase our international competitiveness. It might also be true that the local multiplier effects will be very small. Nevertheless it is worth providing useful work for the long-term young unemployed, even if it lasts for only a year. It is surely better to encourage them to use their energies for constructive rather than for destructive purposes; we must not create a new generation of people without work experience. Even a year's employment is sufficient to produce the self-respect and work habits which young people need if they are to benefit from training programmes for more permanent employment. Thus targeted demand increases are likely to pave the way for the more fundamental structural changes required to increase the number of regular jobs.

Increasing public sector employment

If the long-term unemployed young people were given jobs in the public sector, the net increase in public expenditure would be considerably less than the gross increase, because the payment of unemployment and supplementary benefits would fall and the receipts from income tax and from indirect taxes would rise.[13] Of course, the same would be true for unemployed people over the age of 25, but our concern here is with youth unemployment. In principle, this line of reasoning also applies if jobs were provided by the private sector, but the difference would be that the reduced expenditure on benefits and increased receipts from taxes would be external to the private sector but internal to the public sector.

This difference is used by Britton to devise policies which could use part of the public expenditure on unemployment and supplementary benefits to generate jobs. He suggests that a public sector employment subsidy, confined to full-time employees, should be introduced. The objections to marginal employment subsidies raised in the Economists' Report to the Economic Advisory Council referred to the private sector. Objections to the difficulty of identifying jobs which would be additional to those which would exist without the subsidy are less powerful for the public sector, which should have the administrative control necessary to monitor employment movements. Problems might arise when the public sector organisation competes with the private sector, as Britton recognises, but such competition is less common than between firms in the private sector. Thus, there is a case for introducing a public sector employment subsidy to increase employment in general and youth employment in particular.

Of course, such an employment policy could be thwarted by the public sector trade unions if they decided to press for higher wage rates in response to the increased demand for labour. In 1930, the Economists' Report to the Economic Advisory Council thought that it would be highly optimistic to suppose that wage-earners would refrain from demanding increased wage rates if a general wage subsidy were introduced. Britton also discusses this possibility and stresses the importance of obtaining the agreement of the public sector trade unions to prevent increases in wage rates from absorbing the subsidy. This is yet another example of the crucial importance of trade union attitudes to any government policy to increase employment. It might be difficult to persuade public sector trade unions to allow public sector employment to increase at existing wage levels, rather than to increase public sector wages at existing employment levels, but such a difficulty does not seem to be a sufficient reason for not trying the proposed public sector wage subsidy. After all, it is always possible to reduce the subsidy, or even to eliminate it, if it is thought that public sector wage rates are increasing too quickly.

CONCLUSIONS

Chapter 1 outlined the neo-classical, Keynesian and structuralist approaches to the explanation of the rise of youth unemployment. While none of the available models provides a complete explanation of all aspects of this problem, each provides some insights into some aspects and hence guides us towards appropriate policies to reduce youth unemployment. The neo-classical approach, with its emphasis on wage adjustments bringing the supply and demand for young labour into equilibrium, suggests that relative wages of youngsters have been too high. There is more truth in such an appraisal if it is interpreted widely to include relative non-wage costs in the United Kingdom (Chapters 4, 5 and 7), and relative wages of apprentices in the United Kingdom and Germany (Chapter 6), than if it is restricted to changes in relative wages over time within the United Kingdom (Chapter 3). The standard policy implication of this approach is to remove various impediments to the working of the market for young labour under competition, with the legal framework within which it operates ensuring that such competition is fair. But more important than reducing the relative price of young labour is the raising of its quality by improved education and vocational training. These measures form part of the supply-side policies on education, training, mobility, benefits, taxes, job-start allowances and early retirement, which should help to reduce youth unemployment. However, with over a million under-25 year olds unemployed, supply-side policies are likely to be insufficient by themselves to eliminate it. They have to be combined with appropriate demand-side measures.

In principle, demand-side policies can make a major contribution to the reduction in youth unemployment. The Government has removed any restrictions on the demand for young labour resulting from minimum wage rates in the Wages Council trades, and from employment protection legislation. The gains from such measures, in terms of increased employment, are unlikely to be very large. The Government has also changed tax rates and national insurance contributions to alter relative factor prices in favour of labour and against capital. It could go further by abolishing employers' national insurance contributions. Such a policy could be financed by a payroll tax which could be diminished in line with decreases in the remaining tax allowances on capital expenditure.

The major demand-side policies are normally associated with the Keynesian approach to the reduction of unemployment. Although the traditional Keynesian policy of expanding aggregate demand, coupled with some form of incomes policy, has been rejected by the Conservative Government (and by the Labour opposition), it is still possible to expand demand in selected areas, rather than in the economy as a whole. Such selected expansion is favoured by the Confederation of British Industry, which is a strong supporter of Conservative administrations. The basic idea is that the Government should target demand increases on the young long-term unemployed in our inner cities, thereby minimising the scope for increases in prices and wages. Since such policies are likely to increase output and employment, they merit support. So does the proposal for a public sector employment subsidy.

The policies summarised above are also consistent with the structuralist approach to the reduction of youth unemployment. This rejects the uni-sector, neo-classical, self-equilibrating model of the labour market because of the importance of institutional barriers which create a segmented market for labour. Hence policies to eliminate such barriers, thereby reducing structural imbalance through the union of separate segments into one competitive market, are likely to be supported by the structuralists. Again, targeted demand expansions, which clearly recognise the importance of different market segments, are also consistent with the structuralist approach. It may be possible to expand demand in Sunderland without stimulating inflation, but the same is unlikely to be true for St Albans (Chapter 8). It may not even be true for Inner London, in which case more emphasis must be placed on the supply-side policies, especially education and vocational training.

Whatever policies are adopted, whether on the supply-side, the demand-side, or both, they are likely to require some degree of cooperation between the Government and the relevant trade unions. Such collaboration has occurred on the Youth Training Scheme. Let us hope that this harmony can be extended to other policies. Otherwise we shall be unable to restore the low levels of youth unemployment which prevailed in the 1950s.

DEFINITIONS OF YOUTH AND UNEMPLOYMENT

DEFINITION OF YOUTH

The lower bound of the youth age group is the statutory school-leaving age. This varies over time and between countries and, furthermore, the proportion of a particular population cohort leaving school at the statutory age tends to fall over time as more youths continue their education. In the United Kingdom the statutory school leaving age is now sixteen years; it was raised from fifteen years in September 1972.

The upper bounds in traditional Department of Employment data were 21 years for males and eighteen years for females. The age of majority was reduced from 21 to eighteen years in 1969 and so there is a good case for taking the upper bound of youth as eighteen years for both males and females. At the very least it is consistent with the convention of sex equality. Data on unemployment of males and females using the upper bound of eighteen years is provided by Wells (1983) for the period 1948–81 in his table 10, page 27. In addition he provides data for 18–19 year olds, and hence for males and females under twenty years. Because of the increasing tendency to stay at school after sixteen years, there is a stronger case for using twenty years as the upper bound to youth. The implicit assumption is that by the age of twenty years most of the effects on the labour market of the tendency to stay at school are exhausted. Thus in the regressions of youth unemployment on adult unemployment used in Chapter 2, the upper bound to youth is taken as twenty years.

This is adequate for time-series analysis within one country but when making comparisons between countries different definitions have to be used if only because of different statutory school leaving ages. Thus the lower limit of fifteen years would be taken for Germany and fourteen years if Italy were included in a comparison. Upper limits might differ between countries because of differences in the proportion of young people in full-time education at a particular age. For example, the proportion of 20–24 year olds in full-time education was about 8 per cent in Great Britain in 1975, compared with 12 per cent in Germany and France. There is much to be said for defining youth as below 25 years in the belief that by this age the proportion in full-time education, and differences between different countries, are small enough to regard the full-time educational process as being completed in all countries. Unemployment among young people under 25 years is the variable usually studied in international comparisons of youth unemployment by official organisations such as the United States Bureau of Labor Statistics, the EEC and the OECD. Thus the definition of youth in international comparisons might differ from that used in time-series analysis within the United Kingdom. In practice the definition used is influenced by the type of data available. Providing the statistics of youth unemployment facilitate an understanding of the various unemployment problems experienced by young people, the precise definition of youth is not of crucial importance. What is important is to ensure that like is compared with like in time-series and in cross-section analysis.

DEFINITION OF UNEMPLOYMENT

There are many statistical definitions of unemployment and they may all differ from the standard definition of unemployment in economics. The latter is based on the standard market equilibrium analysis illustrated in chart A1.1. The demand for labour is assumed to be a downward sloping function of the real product wage whereas the supply of labour, at least in the relevant region, is assumed to be upward sloping. The intersection of these two functions gives equilibrium employment at On with equilibrium real product wage Ow. Unemployment arises because the labour market is in disequilibrium; typically the real wage rate is too high at Ow_1 and employment of On_d is demanded giving a shortfall of $n-n_d$. In addition to this amount of unemployment there are n_s-n people who would be willing to work at wage rate Ow_1, but not at wage rate Ow and many of them will appear in the statistics of unemployment.

Some economists believe that the real wage level is rigid downwards, possibly as the result of trade union power. Others would argue that much recorded unemployment is voluntary and that the difference between the market money wage and the unemployment or social security benefit is too small to offset the expenditure of energy (and money) involved in going to work. In their eyes, the statistics of the unemployed are misleading. The true figures are much lower and simply reflect the results of people leaving jobs and searching for others which they will find in due course. Thus the economic definition of youth unemployment will vary with the theoretical model used and could easily differ from the statistical definition.

Thatcher (1976) presents a very clear explanation of the statistics of unemployment compiled for the United Kingdom. The Department of Employment figures used in Chapter 2 were based on the number of people 'capable of and available for work' who registered as unemployed. Those unemployed people who do not register but who claim to be looking for work are counted in the Census of Population and also appear in the data compiled by the EEC Labour Force Survey and by the General Household Survey. The discrepancies between these sources were used by NIESR (1983) to assess the extent to which the long-term upward trend in aggregate unemployment is purely statistical. Once again the definition used is governed by the data available: all that can be done is to note the limitations of the data from an economic point of view.

The figures of the stock of youth unemployment were substantially reduced by Government Special Measures and Training Schemes after 1980, as mentioned in Chapter 2. But there are also several other changes in the official definitions of unemployment which tend to reduce the numbers counted. For aggregate unemployment, the *Unemployment Bulletin* (1986) lists seventeen adjustments to the official time series of unemployment since 1979 which, in its view, reduce the figure of unemployment by more than half a million. A recent change

(March 1986) also affects the estimated unemployment rate because the denominator is now total working population (employed, self-employed, unemployed, HM Forces) which reduces the aggregate unemployment rate by between 1 and 1.5 percentage points. All these changes in statistical definitions in recent years explain why the time-series analysis of youth unemployment in Chapter 2 ends at 1981.

The discussion so far relates to the stock of unemployment, which changes as the result of inflows and outflows. In a recent paper, Pissarides (1986) excluded the flows through Careers Offices and Professional and Executive Recruitment and claimed that the rise in aggregate male employment was due primarily to falling outflows from the unemployment register. However, the official statistics of monthly inflows, which show very little increase 1967–83, exclude those men over 60 who decide to retire from the labour force and this number has increased, as indicated by tables 4.4 and 4A.1. Hence the published inflow rates are biased downwards. Furthermore, on becoming redundant an increasing number of men opt for self-employment, which is another reason why the published inflow rates have not increased very much. Thus the results of Pissarides certainly cannot be applied to youth unemployment. The rate of inflow of young people into the stock of unemployment might well have increased 1967–83. Against this, it might be argued that many youngsters, faced with unemployment, opted to continue their education in the hope that the labour market would improve. This would reduce the inflow rates, and hence tend to reduce the stock figures.

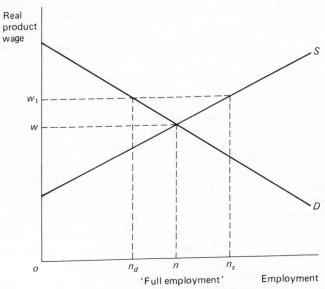

Chart A1.1   Labour market equilibrium

Key: Distance n-n_d in one measure of unemployment. Statistical measures include part of n_s-n. Theory specifies that full employment, On, arises at real product wage Ow when $S = D$. Unemployment results when $w_1 > w$.

RIGID WAGES, TWO-SECTOR MODELS, AND STRUCTURAL UNEMPLOYMENT

1   The assumption that money wage rates are rigid downwards may be justified for the period since 1933. Even in the current economic depression, the official index of wage rates in the United Kingdom has shown no signs of falling. Decreases in average money wage rates were observed in the United Kingdom for 1920–23, and from 1927–33, so it would be wrong to argue that money wages have always been inflexible downwards. However, it is worth noting that real wage rates in consumption units continued to rise 1928–34, in spite of the severe economic depression 1929–33, as shown by Phelps Brown and Hopkins (1950).

2   The assumption that there are two economic sectors in the United Kingdom is an obvious simplification: in practice there are many sectors with barriers of different types and of different 'heights' existing between them, but at least the use of a two-sector model is a closer approximation to the actual United Kingdom economy than is a one-sector model. The sectors might be divided in many ways. For example, we could consider the 'unionised' and 'non-unionised' sectors, following Pemberton (1981) (1984) or we could use the urban–rural dichotomy of Harris and Todaro (1970). Perhaps the insider–outsider dichotomy is more important in the United Kingdom. As shown in Chapters 4 and 5, there has been a remarkable growth in the supply of part-time labour and in the demand for it. The result is that in many firms, especially in the service trades, there is a core of full-time, experienced, possibly skilled labour, which may be classified as 'insiders' or sector 1 workers. Surrounding this core is a periphery of casual, part-time, temporary labour, which may be regarded as 'outsiders' in sector 2. Finally, we could take geographical sectors, with London and South East England as sector 1, and the rest of the country as sector 2. Although sector 1 contains the depressed parts of inner London it remains true that most of the sector is relatively prosperous with the highest house prices in the country. Unemployed workers in North-East England, for example, are unlikely to be able to finance the purchase of a house in sector 1 with proceeds from the sale of their houses in sector 2 and thus cannot seek employment in sector 1. Rented accommodation is not readily available because of rent control. Thus there is a very real obstacle to the mobility of labour.

A two-sector spatial model is probably the easiest to comprehend and to measure but although it is adequate enough to illustrate the underlying economic theory, it is far from constituting an exhaustive explanation of why different parts of the economy can exhibit asymmetrical behaviour in prices, wages, output and employment.

Some industries are not obvious members of one sector, partly because firms and industries move between the two sectors over time in accordance with their relative prosperity. This makes it difficult to submit the structural hypothesis to statistical tests. Indeed, in its extreme form this hypothesis might become irrefutable, and therefore uninteresting, for it can always be argued that any unfavourable statistical results arise because the two sectors have not been measured correctly. But without adopting such an extreme position, it remains true that the structural explanation of unemployment might be relevant if an expansion of aggregate demand tended to increase imports and raise prices and wages in whatever occupations, industries and locations compose sector 1, without substantially reducing unemployment in sector 2. That is, the Keynesian 'bottlenecks' are not isolated features of the economy but are common enough to thwart a Keynesian expansionist policy.

Clearly, the two-sector model rests on persistent disequilibrium and the obvious question arises, 'Why not cut real wages in sector 2 sufficiently to remove all unemployment in this sector?' There is more than one reason why equilibrium is unlikely to be regained in this way. It is possible that real wages in sector 2 are already low and any further reduction will make the excess over unemployment benefit even smaller and hence reduce the supply of labour and increase the statistics of unemployment. The standard counter to this effect, namely reducing real unemployment benefits, might not be feasible from the political point of view.

An alternative explanation for the continuing disequilibrium is that the unemployed in sector 2 prefer to continue to queue for jobs in sector 1 because the expected wage and prospects in sector 1 are so much higher than those in sector 2. Moreover, if they take jobs in sector 2 they might miss a job opportunity in sector 1 because they are not available for employment or because job search is more effective while they are unemployed. The alternative explanation is reasonable when the two sectors are spatial, such as the urban–rural, or London, South-East England–rest of the United Kingdom, for those who wish to obtain jobs in sector 1 stand more chance of doing so if they move to sector 1 and queue for jobs there.

3   The measure of structural unemployment used by Jackman and Roper (1985) is:

$$SU = \tfrac{1}{2} U \sum_{i}^{n} |\hat{u}_i - \hat{v}_i|, \quad i = 1 \dots, n$$

where U is aggregate unemployment, $\hat{u}_i$ and $\hat{v}_i$ denote the ith sector's share of aggregate unemployment and vacancies respectively, and SU is the definition of structural unemployment.

In empirical work on structural unemployment, the number of sectors, n, is usually greater than 2. Their conclusion that structural unemployment, as measured by SU, is unimportant is based on $n = 9$ for regions, or $m = 24$ for industries. The value of n is governed by the available data.

Let us define $x_i = \hat{u}_i - \hat{v}_i$. The mean deviation of x_i is given by

$$\delta = (1/n) \sum_{i}^{n} |x_i| \qquad\qquad \text{A2.1}$$

Array x_i in ascending order and let there be n_1 positive values and $n_2 = n - n_1$ values of zero or less. The arithmetic mean is zero,

$$\bar{x} = \sum^{n} x_i/n = \sum^{n} (\hat{u}_i - \hat{v}_i)/n = 0 \qquad \text{A2.2}$$

since $\Sigma\hat{u}_i = \Sigma\hat{v}_i = 1$,

and

$$n\delta = 2\sum_{1}^{n_1} x_i = -2\sum_{n_2}^{0} x_i \qquad \text{A2.3}$$

because the positive values of x_i must balance the negative values of x_i to give $\bar{x} = 0$. Hence the Jackman–Roper measure is

$$SU = Un\delta/2 = U\sum_{0}^{n_1} x_i = -\sum_{n_2}^{0} Ux_i \qquad \text{A2.4}$$

or aggregate unemployment multiplied by the sum of the positive differences (or by the negative of the sum of the negative differences) between the sector shares of unemployment and of vacancies.

For a normal distribution $\delta = 0.8\sigma_i$, where σ_i is the standard deviation of x_i. If the x_i are approximately normally distributed across the sectors, then

$$SU = 0.4Un\sigma_i \qquad \text{A2.5}$$

or 40 per cent of aggregate unemployment multiplied by the number of sectors, multiplied by σ_i. The SU measure increases as n increases, but how does σ_i vary?

Without loss of generality, let us suppose that there are m local labour markets in the ith sector, with x_{ij} denoting the difference between the shares of unemployment and of vacancies in the jth local labour market in the ith sector. Now x_i is the sum, not the mean, of x_{ij}:

$$x_i = \sum_{j}^{m} x_{ij} = (1/U)\sum_{j}^{m} U_{ij} - (1/V)\sum_{j}^{m} V_{ij} = (U_i/U) - (V_i/V) \qquad \text{A2.6}$$

If the m local labour markets are chosen so that they are independent,

$$x_i^2 = \sum_{j}^{m} x_{ij}^2.$$

Consider how the term σ_i in A2.5 changes as the n sectors are disaggregated into nm local labour markets.
Now $n\sigma_i = \sqrt{n}\,\sqrt{\Sigma_i x_i^2}$ before disaggregation. Afterwards we have

$$mn\sigma_{ij} = \sqrt{nm}\,\sqrt{\Sigma_i x_i^2} = n\sigma_i\sqrt{m} \qquad \text{A2.7}$$

Thus the SU measure is multiplied by $\sqrt{m}$ and can be increased simply by reducing the size of local labour markets and thereby increasing their number. This makes SU measures largely arbitrary.

In their footnote 11, page 54, Jackman and Roper (1985) show that they are well aware of the problems created by disaggregation but they argue that 46 per cent of the variation of local unemployment rates is attributable to variations between the standard regions. But this merely means that 54 per cent is due to variations between local labour markets within regions. The within region variation is more important than the between region variation. Unfortunately, there are no data on vacancies for local labour markets hence the within region variation of x_{ij} cannot be calculated. However, using equation A2.7 it can be seen that if m and n are constant over time we may use changes in σ_i as a guide to changes in σ_{ij}. While n is constant, m probably falls because improvements in private transport increase the size of the local labour market. Dividing (A2.7) by $n\sqrt{m}$ gives

$$\sigma_{ij}\sqrt{m} = \sigma_i \qquad \text{A2.8}$$

and it is clear that with falling values of m, σ_{ij} could increase while σ_i remained much the same. Thus changes in σ_i cannot be used to measure changes in σ_{ij}, the measure of structural unemployment at the level of the local labour market.

The use of σ_i highlights the spatial dispersion of U and V. Jackman and Roper (1985) are well aware that their concept of structural unemployment is a narrow one, but they argue that labour is mobile between industries (providing a regional move is not involved) and that industrial restructuring is not a major cause of the rise in unemployment. An alternative view is that the absence of sufficient industrial restructuring is a major cause of the rise in unemployment; we have not adapted quickly enough to changes in world markets. All regions share this resistance to change. In a world context, all United Kingdom regions might have structural unemployment: the dispersion of such measures between regions may be small, or not increasing very rapidly, but the mean is high by world standards. The distributional coalitions, or vested interests, which block change also hinder possible solutions such as the depreciation of the real exchange rate.

TRENDS IN UNEMPLOYMENT

The upward trend in aggregate unemployment has attracted the attention of many economists, for example Brittan (1975), Roberthall (1982), Matthews, Feinstein and Odling-Smee (1982), Nickell (1982), NIESR (1983), Ermisch (1983), Gordon (1985), Britton (1986). Although these authors did not distinguish between youth and adult unemployment, the similarity of the trends in charts 2.3 and and 2.4 suggests that their explanations of the upward trend in aggregate unemployment are relevant to the explanation of the upward trend in youth unemployment. Indeed, as noted in Chapter 2 there is some evidence to support the view that whatever explains total unemployment also explains youth unemployment. After all youth unemployment is an important component part of aggregate unemployment. It is therefore necessary to review their explanations of the upward trend in aggregate unemployment.

Matthews *et al.* (1982) cover an earlier period and their analysis stops in 1973. They are particularly interested in cycles of unemployment but note that 'Within the period 1951–64 there was a mild but downward trend in the pressure of demand for labour, as measured by both unemployment and vacancies' (p.91). The steeper rise in unemployment in the period 1965–73 is attributed to an 'increase in the output elasticity of employment, together with an increase in the degree of mismatch in the labour market, and possibly a continuation of a trend weakening in the demand for labour relative to the supply' (p.91). The increase in the output-elasticity of employment in the second period is probably linked with reductions in labour hoarding and possibly with higher social security benefits. In a sense unemployment breeds unemployment: if employers are confident that they can always recruit additional labour in times of high unemployment they are more likely to run down the 'precautionary' stocks of labour in times of downswing, thereby accentuating the increase in unemployment, although reducing the extent of 'overmanning'.

Ermisch (1983) (p.129) relates the upward trend in unemployment rates to potential labour supply, and in particular notes, 'a new trend emerged in the postwar period, which had a major influence on the size and composition of the labour supply throughout the postwar years; the growing participation of women in paid employment'. He also suggests that the 'shakeout of labour' 1967–70 was partly a result of redundancy payments legislation in 1965 and 1969, of the selective employment tax in 1966 and of the abolition of resale price maintenance in 1964. This legislation tended to increase youth unemployment because young people were more vulnerable, and were also more abundant because of the high birth rates after the war. Moreover, this increase in youth unemployment reinforced the tendency for more young people to continue their education beyond the statutory age limit and thus tended to reduce their labour participation rates. He also claims that hourly earnings of young men continued to rise relatively to those of adult men, in spite of the entry of the 'baby boom' generation into the labour market after 1975 which led to increases in the supply of young men.[1]

An official explanation of the long-term upward trend in unemployment was provided by the Government in its reply to the Report from the Select Committee of the House of Lords on Unemployment (1982). It stated that unemployment had risen unevenly but persistently over the previous twenty years linked with our long-standing and widely recognised problems of low profitability, poor labour productivity, failure to invest adequately in new products, skills and processes and failure to adapt quickly enough to economic changes. Among the many reasons for these shortcomings were excessive pay increases, entrenched restrictive labour practices, inefficient use of new capital investment and lack of response to new market opportunities. All these long-term difficulties were accentuated by massive increases in the price of oil since 1973 and the subsequent worldwide recession.

The Government rejected the claim that increasing aggregate demand was the answer to mass unemployment; 'Suppositions that unemployment can be overcome simply by increasing monetary demand, and that those who have a job accordingly need not moderate their expectations of higher incomes for the sake of those without one, offer no solution; they have indeed done much to create the problem'.[2]

In his study of the equilibrium between the outflow and inflow of unemployment, Nickell (1982) concentrated on measuring the effect of secular rather than cyclical variables. These included profitability, the proportion working in the production sector, the replacement ratio, employment protection legislation (unfair dismissals), pressure on unemployed to obtain work and the decline in direct demand. Even so, the most important determinant over the period 1969–77 was 'unexplained trend' which contributed 1.41 percentage points to the observed increase of 3.77 percentage points. The increase in the unemployment of young males under twenty over the same period was nearer 12 percentage points. The increase 1974–7 was more pronounced than in earlier depressions. The increase after 1979 seems in line with the earlier upward trend but because of the effects of the various government special measures on youth unemployment statistics, we cannot be certain about this.

All the above studies are traditional in the sense that they seek to explain deterministic trend in terms of systematic forces. But perhaps we should view macroeconomic time series as random walks with drift, and reject the concept of a deterministic trend. This is the approach of Nelson and Plosser (1982) and of Nelson and Kang (1984), which might not be regarded as traditional even though its emphasis on stochastic shocks in economic time series has a long history. It seems likely that economic shocks, such as the OPEC oil price increases, have contributed to the secular rise in youth unemployment and are consistent with the model of a random walk with drift. Nevertheless, in the present book the emphasis is on the systematic rather than the stochastic causes of the long-term rise in youth unemployment.

LABOUR FORCE SURVEY DATA

Table A4.1. *Labour Force Survey data for Great Britain on persons aged 16–19, 20–24 living in private households, Spring each year, thousands*

	In employment[a]	In employment full-time[b]	In employment part-time[b]	Un-employed[c]	Inactive students[d]	Others[e]	Total
Age 16–19							
1979 M	1,067	1,002	41	156	478	37	1,738
F	931	838	75	155	489	119	1,694
1981 M	1,012	840	122	304	474	37	1,827
F	932	727	181	245	481	110	1,768
1983 M	964	764	118	316	522	51	1,853
F	889	623	203	237	527	133	1,775
1984 M	1,003	797	169	284	488	33	1,807
F	915	655	242	230	466	129	1,740
1985[f] M	1,018	803	172	257	450	38	1,763
F	948	663	266	207	413	133	1,702
Age 20–24							
1979 M	1,679	1,578	12	120	125	27	1,951
F	1,202	1,056	117	115	81	486	1,884
1981 M	1,563	1,417	18	291	158	35	2,047
F	1,234	1,058	121	175	108	492	2,009
1983 M	1,562	1,521	30	361	155	68	2,146
F	1,274	1,128	136	197	114	531	2,115
1984 M	1,626	1,575	47	377	158	63	2,225
F	1,311	1,126	182	227	114	525	2,174
1985[f] M	1,708	1,639	68	357	138	77	2,28
F	1,361	1,165	196	210	96	550	2,218

Source: House of Commons (1986) *Parliamentary Debates*, 24 June, 1986, pp. 113–16.

[a] Includes those who did not state if they worked full- or part-time, and those on a government employment scheme or, in 1979 and 1981 only, who were self-employed and not asked if the work was full- or part-time.

[b] The definition of full-time and part-time is based on the respondent's own assessment and n on the number of hours worked.

[c] Those without a job and looking for work in the reference week, or prevented from seeking wo by temporary sickness or holiday, or waiting for the results of a job application or waiting start a job they had already obtained.

[d] Inactive students are those students not classified as in employment or unemployed. Those w reported doing paid work are classified as in employment. In 1979 and 1981 all students w said they were seeking work were classified as unemployed, but in later years those who sa they were seeking work but not available to start a job because they had to complete their educati were classified as inactive.

[e] Mainly for females looking after house or home, and sick and disabled.

[f] The figures for 1985 are preliminary estimates.

OCCUPIED POPULATION BY AGE, SEX AND INDUSTRY

Table A5.1 classifies the labour force by age, sex and industry in 1961, 1966 and 1971, thus providing data between the Census years 1951 and 1981 in table 4.4. It supplements the various tables compiled by Ermisch (1983) and by Matthews *et al.* (1982) in their analyses of the long-term changes in the labour market.

Ermisch notes in his Chapter 4 that during the early 1950s labour demand grew more quickly than the demographic sources of supply. There was no growth in the supply of males because of earlier fertility movements, wartime mortality and decreases in participation. This encouraged employers to hire more married women in the age group 35–54, who often had had work experience in the war. International immigration also made a positive contribution during 1956–61. In the early 1960s two thirds of the increase in the labour force was supplied by married women aged 35–54. Since then the labour market has been less buoyant, especially in the 1970s and 1980s, but women's participation in the labour force continued to grow, partly as a result of the shift in the industrial and occupational distribution of employment in favour of jobs for women, and partly because of the growing importance of part-time employment.

Matthews *et al.* discuss in their Chapter 3 the long-term increase in female participation rates associated with the fall in family size, fall in average age of marriage, increases in family income aspirations and changes in attitudes to working married women which were hastened by two wars. They also note that labour shortages, which persisted for a while after the Second World War, were met in part by the employment of more women, particularly as part-time workers. In the period 1951–64 there were net excess demands for skilled labour at cyclical peaks but there was no chronic excess demand for labour as a whole, as there was in the postwar years before 1951.

Table A5.1. *Occupied population by age, sex and industry, Great Britain, 1961, 1966 and 1971, thousands*

	15	16–19	20–24	25–59	60+	All ages
1961						
Males						
Agriculture	12.7	65.7	66.2	509.5	106.4	760.5
Energy	7.5	52.8	80.8	804.5	91.7	1,037.3
Manufacturing	74.8	431.1	521.4	4,256.8	535.0	5,819.1
Construction	23.7	146.8	171.8	1,091.7	97.7	1,531.7
Transport and communications	6.9	60.0	109.8	1,116.9	152.9	1,446.5
Finance	0.8	25.6	29.2	249.7	31.2	336.5
Distribution	30.6	147.7	128.9	1,175.4	199.5	1,682.0
Services	24.6	206.2	324.7	2,142.8	363.4	3,061.7
Not stated	1.1	7.6	8.8	48.1	7.4	73.1
All industries	182.8	1,143.6	1,441.5	11,395.4	1,585.2	15,748.5
Females						
Agriculture	1.5	10.9	9.4	62.6	10.5	94.9
Energy	0.7	8.8	11.7	38.8	2.1	62.1
Manufacturing	74.1	416.9	366.1	1,592.9	113.4	2,563.5
Construction	1.4	11.4	10.4	41.4	3.5	68.1
Transport and communications	3.5	31.5	37.3	145.6	8.5	226.4
Finance	4.3	67.2	48.7	106.3	8.8	235.3
Distribution	59.8	236.6	165.6	944.8	99.8	1,506.6
Services	28.7	266.8	325.3	1,929.4	252.0	2,802.2
Not stated	1.0	4.7	4.4	18.0	3.1	31.1
All industries	174.8	1,054.8	978.9	4,879.9	501.8	7,590.2
Males and females						
Agriculture	14.2	76.6	75.6	572.1	116.9	855.4
Energy	8.2	61.6	92.5	843.3	93.7	1,099.4
Manufacturing	148.9	848.0	887.5	5,849.7	648.4	8,382.6
Construction	25.1	158.2	182.2	1,133.1	101.2	1,599.8
Transport and communications	10.4	91.5	147.1	1,262.5	161.4	1,672.9
Finance	5.1	92.9	77.9	356.0	40.0	571.8
Distribution	90.4	384.3	294.5	2,120.2	299.3	3,188.7
Services	53.3	473.0	650.0	4,072.2	615.4	5,863.9
Not stated	2.1	12.3	13.2	66.1	10.5	104.2
All industries	357.6	2,198.4	2,420.4	16,275.3	2,087.0	23,338.7

Table A5.1. *Occupied population by age, sex and industry, Great Britain, 1961,
1966 and 1971, thousands—(contd)*

	15	16–19	20–24	25–59	60+	All ages
1966						
Males						
Agriculture	7.9	55.2	56.3	424.3	104.1	647.8
Energy	3.6	53.5	67.1	682.0	93.1	899.3
Manufacturing	48.2	472.0	577.4	4,124.8	569.6	5,792.0
Construction	17.7	198.9	220.3	1,209.3	133.3	1,779.5
Transport and						
communications	3.3	65.8	110.3	1,024.5	142.1	1,346.0
Finance	0.4	30.8	43.3	247.6	39.3	361.4
Distribution	25.5	164.3	150.4	1,030.6	210.9	1,581.7
Services	19.9	246.9	333.3	2,114.1	412.4	3,126.6
Not stated	0.6	4.7	5.4	24.1	4.8	39.6
All industries	127.1	1,292.1	1,563.8	10,881.3	1,709.6	15,573.8
Females						
Agriculture	0.9	9.7	8.9	82.6	12.0	114.1
Energy	0.4	10.3	11.8	46.8	2.9	72.2
Manufacturing	50.3	436.3	344.2	1,661.3	141.0	2,633.1
Construction	1.2	16.2	14.7	62.2	6.0	100.3
Transport and						
communications	2.3	36.3	37.1	171.9	14.4	262.0
Finance	2.6	85.2	68.4	124.0	14.0	294.2
Distribution	42.7	259.4	164.2	1,060.4	136.7	1,663.4
Services	20.5	312.2	373.5	2,370.0	352.6	3,428.8
Not stated	0.4	4.8	3.6	14.9	3.1	26.8
All industries	121.3	1,170.4	1,026.4	5,594.1	682.7	8,594.9
Males and females						
Agriculture	8.8	64.9	65.2	506.9	116.1	761.9
Energy	4.0	63.8	78.9	728.8	96.0	971.5
Manufacturing	98.5	908.3	921.6	5,786.1	710.6	8,425.1
Construction	18.9	215.1	235.0	1,271.5	139.3	1,879.8
Transport and						
communications	5.5	102.1	147.4	1,196.4	156.5	1,608.0
Finance	3.0	116.0	111.7	371.6	53.3	655.6
Distribution	68.2	423.7	314.6	2,091.0	347.6	3,245.1
Services	40.4	559.1	706.8	4,484.1	765.0	6,555.4
Not stated	1.0	9.5	9.2	39.0	7.9	66.4
All industries	248.4	2,462.5	2,590.2	16,475.4	2,392.3	24,168.7

Table A5.1. *Occupied population by age, sex and industry, Great Britain, 1961, 1966 and 1971, thousands—(contd)*

	15	16–19	20–24	25–59	60+	All ages
1971						
Males						
Agriculture	5.1	35.8	47.3	349.6	86.8	524.6
Energy	2.5	33.0	57.6	517.2	65.4	675.6
Manufacturing	31.2	384.7	651.2	4,096.6	556.9	5,720.5
Construction	9.3	119.1	216.1	1,097.7	129.9	1,572.0
Transport and communications	2.0	49.8	128.9	992.7	124.8	1,298.2
Finance	0.5	25.7	66.4	331.9	50.3	474.7
Distribution	17.5	120.7	161.2	946.3	208.3	1,453.9
Services	13.4	194.3	406.1	2,191.5	422.2	3,227.6
Not stated	2.2	10.8	12.7	50.2	8.4	84.3
All industries	83.6	973.9	1,747.3	10,573.7	1,653.0	15,031.6
Females						
Agriculture	0.6	5.8	7.2	82.8	13.7	110.1
Energy	0.2	8.2	13.9	53.0	2.8	78.1
Manufacturing	33.8	291.8	344.4	1,610.7	134.6	2,415.3
Construction	0.6	10.6	16.7	62.8	6.4	97.1
Transport and communications	1.4	26.5	45.5	178.8	13.5	265.7
Finance	2.7	91.1	119.2	242.1	22.3	477.4
Distribution	28.8	175.4	163.9	1,042.7	151.2	1,562.0
Services	15.1	233.1	443.1	2,555.8	355.1	3,602.1
Not stated	2.2	9.6	9.5	59.4	12.4	93.1
All industries	85.6	852.2	1,163.3	5,888.1	711.9	8,701.1
Males and females						
Agriculture	5.7	41.6	54.5	432.4	100.5	634.7
Energy	2.7	41.2	71.5	570.2	68.2	753.7
Manufacturing	65.0	676.5	995.6	5,707.3	691.5	8,135.8
Construction	9.9	129.7	232.8	1,160.5	136.3	1,669.1
Transport and communications	3.4	76.3	174.4	1,171.5	138.3	1,563.9
Finance	3.2	116.8	185.6	574.0	72.6	952.1
Distribution	46.3	296.1	325.1	1,989.0	359.5	3,015.9
Services	28.5	427.4	849.2	4,747.3	777.3	6,829.7
Not stated	4.4	20.4	22.2	109.6	20.8	177.4
All industries	169.2	1,826.1	2,910.6	16,461.8	2,364.9	23,732.7

NOTES

I THE RISE OF YOUTH UNEMPLOYMENT

1 See Prais (1986a, p. 98). The definitions of youth and of unemployment are discussed in Appendix 1. Chapter 2 contains comparisons of the upward trends in youth and adult unemployment.

2 In its summary of the various theories of the causes of unemployment, the Select Committee of the House of Lords on Unemployment (1982, Volume 1 – Report, Chapter 4) provides a more detailed classification of the standard economic theories. Thus its special mention of monetarist explanations, and of rational expectations, would be included here under neo-classical economic models, its stagnation thesis and 'New Cambridge' approach under Keynesian models, and its technological change under structural unemployment. Its separate consideration of Marx, unemployment and the capitalist crisis has no counterpart here. For that matter, the fascist solution to mass unemployment, which achieved some popularity in the 1930s, is also excluded.

3 This does not imply that all the Government's policies on youth unemployment follow the neo-classical approach. The important Youth Training Scheme is included in the section on the structuralist approach. The Community Programme could be linked to the policy of targeted increases in demand considered in Chapter 9 and may be classified as a Keynesian approach. Some policies, such as the marginal wage subsidies in the Young Workers' Scheme, New Workers' Scheme and the Job-Start Allowance appear to violate the neo-classical approach.

4 The West Midlands area provides an excellent example of a current excess demand for skilled labour in the midst of high unemployment. See Lewis and Armstrong (1986).

5 The Keynesian approach emphasises *quantity* adjustments, rather than *price* adjustments, to remove the disequilibrium. It is not disputed that, following an expansion of aggregate demand, bottlenecks might arise in some markets for skilled labour and that wages, and hence prices, might increase in such markets. However, the extent of such price and wage adjustments is in dispute. For example, consider the criticism of Hayek (1967):

> 'That so long as a state of general unemployment prevails, in the sense that unused resources of *all* kinds exist, monetary expansion can be only beneficial, few people will deny. But such a state of general unemployment is something rather exceptional, and it is by no means evident that a policy which will be beneficial in such a state will also always and necessarily be so in the kind of intermediate position in which an economic system finds itself most of the time, when significant unemployment is confined to certain industries, occupations or localities.'

6   For example, Doeringer and Piore (1971) suggested that there is a dual
    labour market. The *primary sector* consists of a series of internal labour markets
    in which the pricing and allocation of labour is governed by administrative
    rules and procedures of the firms concerned. The *secondary sector* contains
    (a) unstructured markets for labour, such as domestic work or dishwashing,
    (b) secondary internal labour markets, such as menial jobs in hospitals,
    which have many entry points for labour, and (c) secondary jobs attached
    to primary internal labour markets, such as those in the foundry of a machine
    tool company.

7   Morris and Sinclair (1985) provide a valuable assessment of one-sector neo-
    classical and Keynesian models of unemployment. They regard structural
    explanations of unemployment as relatively uncontentious and argue that
    policies to reduce structural unemployment are consistent with either neo-
    classical or Keynesian analysis. But the fact that the structural approach
    raises less contentious issues does not mean that it is less important than
    the neo-classical or the Keynesian analysis of unemployment.

8   Lindbeck and Snower (1985) also concentrate on one-sector neo-classical
    and Keynesian models. However, they have a most helpful summary of
    insider-outsider theory which may be regarded as a two-sector model. For
    various reasons, those already employed (insiders) do not have to pay too
    much attention to competition from the unemployed (outsiders). Indeed,
    for a time, the wages of insiders can increase more quickly than prices without
    significantly reducing their employment; they are in sector 1. Wage inflation
    in sector 1 can coexist with mass unemployment in sector 2.

9   See for example Atkinson and Meager (1986) and IDS Study 374 (1986).

2   THE TIME SERIES OF YOUTH UNEMPLOYMENT

1   The direct effects of all the special employment and training measures on
    the figures in the unemployment register are estimated and discussed in
    the *National Institute Economic Review*, February 1985.

2   The separate figures for young males and females 1952–81 are based on
    various assumptions. See footnotes in Wells (1983), pp. 89–95. It should
    be noted that the denominator of the youth unemployment rate, giving the
    total young working population, was recorded annually 1952–72 from the
    National Insurance card count. For 1975, 1977 and 1981 estimates were
    made from the Labour Force Survey. Linear interpolation was used for
    the intervening years. Other techniques were used to estimate figures for
    1973 and 1974.

3   With P_{at} denoting the economically active population at time t, we may
    write $\log_e P_{at} = \alpha_1 + \beta_1 t$, and $\log_e U_t = \alpha_2 + \beta_2 t$ where U_t denotes the unem-
    ployed at time t. Hence the trend in the unemployment rate is given by
    $\log_e (U_t/P_{at}) = \alpha_3 + \beta_3 t$, with $\alpha_3 = \alpha_2 - \alpha_1$ and $\beta_3 = \beta_2 - \beta_1$.
    There are good precedents for using a logarithmic scale. At least since

the days of Malthus, economists have regarded the growth of the human population as being geometric rather than arithmetic and hence a logarithmic transformation is appropriate. More recently Wells (1983), tables 17, 18, equation D6 pp. 59–60 included equations with the logarithm of the unemployment percentage, after first differencing, as the dependent variable. Again another influential paper by Nickell (1982) used the logarithms of the outflow–unemployment ratio and the inflow–employment ratio as dependent variables and, furthermore, analysed their trends.

Nickell used quarterly data 1967(1) to 1977(4). Unfortunately, it is not possible to analyse the inflows into, and outflows from, the stock of youth unemployment for our time period, 1952–81. The most relevant data start in January 1978 and relate to flows through Careers Offices and Professional and Executive Recruitment which are dominated by school and college leavers. See Hughes (1982). This series could be used to approximate the inflows and outflows of young people (under 22) from the stock of unemployment, otherwise no breakdown of flows by age is published. Nickell was concerned with aggregate inflows and outflows and the data he used excluded flows through Careers Offices and Professional and Executive Recruitment.

4 The deterministic trends discussed in Chapter 2 should not be used to forecast youth unemployment in the future if only because their economic appraisal is designed to reveal appropriate methods for reversing them.

5 Some people might argue that in the absence of the government's special youth training schemes and the like, the proportion of young people unemployed would approximate 100 per cent in due course. The main reason for making such an appalling forecast is to make sure it does not happen by persuading the government and other economic agents to undertake economic policies which will 'bend the trend'.

6 U_{YM} refers to males aged twenty years or less, U_{AM} to males over twenty years.

7 The sequential Chow tests apply F-tests to the recursive residuals, see Harvey (1976, 1981). The computer program used also provides cusum tests based on the cumulative sums of squares of the recursive residuals, but in view of Fisher's (1980) paper showing the equivalence of these tests, only the sequential and ordinary Chow tests are reported here.

3   YOUTH UNEMPLOYMENT AND RELATIVE WAGES IN THE UNITED KINGDOM: A SURVEY OF THE EVIDENCE

1 The Select Committee of the House of Lords on Unemployment (1982, page 36, paragraph 5.12) regarded 1966 as marking a break. 'Mid-1966 is an obvious turning point. The latest in a series of balance of payments crises led to the introduction of a package of tax increases and expenditure reductions. The effect of these measures on expectations was at least as important as their direct influence on the economy. They represented the explicit abandonment of the growth ambitions of the early 1960s. Unemployment rose during the rest of 1966 at a rate which had not been seen since the immediate postwar years. Moreover, the new levels of unemployment were seen as

unavoidable, if undesired, by-products of other economic policies; whereas in previous recessions similar levels of unemployment had turned reductions in unemployment into the first priority of economic policy.'

2   If a firm is choosing inputs so that it maximises its output for any given input cost (the 'primal'), it must also be minimising its input costs for that particular output (the 'dual'). The two statements are simply different ways of expressing the same aim of optimising subject to constraints, but in practice it might be easier to measure a cost function than a production function. For an exposition of duality theory, see Deaton and Muellbauer (1980). Their discussion of systems of demand equations is directly relevant to the estimation of systems of demand equations for labour by Abowd *et al.* (1981).

3   There are several generalisations of the familiar log-linear Cobb-Douglas production function. One generalisation is the transcendental logarithmic function which is quadratic in the logarithms of variables. That is, it adds the cross-products and squares of the logarithms of variables to the Cobb-Douglas form. A very helpful discussion of such 'translog' cost functions is provided by Roy and Wenban-Smith (1983).

4   Those who are quite prepared to transfer girls from shops to building sites, or to the coal mines, might prefer to use j to denote skilled labour and k to denote unskilled. While it is possible to substitute the jth type of labour for the kth, the reverse substitution is impossible. It is true that unskilled labour can be trained, but then it is no longer of the kth type.

The Slutsky symmetry conditions emerge from the mathematics of constrained optimisation in consumer demand theory when an individual maximises his utility subject to his budget constraint. It is clear that this result cannot be extended to the demand for all types of labour by all firms. But the asymmetry of different types of labour is more than an aggregation problem; even at the level of an individual firm, unskilled cannot be substituted for skilled labour at least in the short run. In the long run, it might be able to change its methods of production and substitute unskilled for skilled labour, but then it moves to a different production function. The labour market differs from the goods market in many ways and there is no reason why the full rigour of consumer demand theory should carry over to the theory of the demand for labour.

5   General macroeconomic forces are excluded from the variables in each of the time-series demand equations in the system and hence might influence the disturbance terms, which might be correlated across equations. The estimation technique of 'seemingly unrelated regressions', or SURE, allows for such correlation. It also allows for constraints across equations, such as those arising from the Slutsky symmetry conditions, and gives more efficient estimates of the coefficients even if the disturbance terms are not correlated across equations. Several econometrics texbooks explain SURE, for example Harvey (1981).

4   THE SUPPLY OF YOUNG LABOUR

1   The occupied population excludes the unemployed. It equals the sum of

those working full-time or part-time, including the self-employed. While it is convenient to include tables 4.3 and 4.4 in this section, it must be emphasised that the data are the combined outcome of supply and demand influences and are not the result of supply only.

Wells (1983, table D16, p. 94) shows that the number of females under twenty years who were registered as unemployed (including school-leavers) increased from 19.9 thousand in 1952 to 216.4 thousand in 1981.

Matthews *et al.* (1982), table 3.15, page 73, show that the proportion of female part-timers in total female employment increased from 12.1 per cent in 1951 to 28.6 per cent in 1964, and to 34.6 per cent in 1973. A more recent study, by Gomulka and Stern (1986, page 24) shows that trends in the proportion of females working part-time depend on the number of hours used to define part-time work. If 30 hours a week mark the dividing line between full- and part-time work, the percentage of female part-time workers fluctuated between 55.6 and 51.2 per cent over the decade 1970/71 to 1980/81 without any clear trend, although it increased to 58.6 per cent by 1982/3. If 23 hours a week mark the dividing line, the percentage of female part-time workers increased from 36.5 per cent in the period 1970/71 to 1973/4 to 38.5 per cent in the years 1974/5 to 1979/80, with a further increase to 1982/3.

Manley and Sawbridge (1980) show that in 1977 some 41 per cent of the female labour force worked part-time in the United Kingdom, compared with 28 per cent in Germany, 18 per cent in France, 28 per cent in the Netherlands and 12 per cent in Italy. The OECD (1983) *Employment Outlook*, September 1983, estimates these percentages for eighteen countries in 1981. In the United Kingdom some 37.1 per cent of females in employment had part-time jobs, with thirteen countries (including the United States) having lower percentages of part-time work. The four countries with higher percentages of part-timers were Denmark (43.6), Netherlands (45.2), Norway (53.6), Sweden (46.4). In the United Kingdom part-time work is defined as less than 30 hours a week, but for the Netherlands it is less than 40 hours a week (or less than normal hours), and for Sweden and Norway it is less than 35 hours a week.

Neubourg (1985, table 1, p. 560) shows that with a 35-hours upper limit for part-time work, the United Kingdom had higher proportions of part-timers than France, West Germany and the Netherlands in 1973 and 1981. But he explains that the Labour Force Sample Survey (LFSS) data on which his other tables are based do not use a single cut-off point between part-time and full-time work. He also shows that the difference between the LFSS calculations of part-time work and the single cut-off point of 35 hours is greatest for the United Kingdom.

The persistence of the Victorian 'practical man's' bias against formal technical training is discussed in detail by Barnett (1986). For example, in January 1942 the Deputy Director of the Ministry of Labour and National Service was complaining of industry's ingrained prejudice against institutional training for higher grades of skilled labour, for example 'setters, tool makers and the like' (p. 211). Again 'In Manchester in 1942, where there was an acute shortage of tool-setters, fewer than a quarter of the available high-grade places at the government training centre had been taken up, and none by local firms' (p. 211). The Ministry of Aircraft Production found employees reluctant to train seriously (p. 211). Vickers-Armstrong was particularly weak on training (p. 211).

6 The submission of Symons and Walker (1986) was not the only evidence leading the House of Lords Select Committee to conclude, 'The Committee find convincing the argument that such a system (i.e. transferable allowances) would create a substantial disincentive to wives in seeking paid employment' (page 29, paragraph 84). Evidence from the following supported this view; City Women's Network (page 125), The Fawcett Society (page 127), Dr Hilary Land (page 138), National Board of Catholic Women (page 143), National Labour Women's Committee (page 146), National and Local Government Officers Association (page 152), Basic Income Group (page 157), TUC General Council (page 168).

7 Wells (1983), table D16, page 94.

8 A neo-classical economist might claim that the increase in the supply of young labour would not have increased youth unemployment if wages were flexible. A Keynesian economist might argue that if aggregate demand had been increased sufficiently there would not have been such a huge rise in youth unemployment. Thus the precise effect of the increase in the supply of young labour varies with the theoretical model which is thought to be the closest approximation to the economy. But whichever model is chosen the large increase in the supply of young labour must have had a depressing effect on the labour market; it increased the size of wage changes necessary in a neo-classical model and increased the necessary injection of aggregate demand in a Keynesian model, in order to avoid the high level of youth unemployment. Some statistical evidence of the effects of the increase in the numbers of young people on youth unemployment is provided by OECD (1980, table 15, page 51) for the period 1959–79. More recent evidence may be found in OECD (1986, chapter V, page 106–127).

5 THE DEMAND FOR YOUNG LABOUR

1 For example, Artis, Bladen-Hovell, Karakitos, and Dwolatzky, (1984) Hall, Henry, Markandya, and Pemberton (1985), Saville and Gardiner (1986).

2 References to some surveys of the many explanations of unemployment are given in the notes to Chapter 1.

3 See Makeham (1980), table 1, p. 67.

4 The percentage of the female population of working age, and under twenty years, in either post-compulsory education or the armed forces increased from 13.8 in 1952 to 32 per cent in 1983, as shown by Wells (1983, table D21, page 99).

5 Table 4.4 shows that the percentage of female part-time clerks increased from 3.1 per cent in 1951 to 18.6 per cent in 1981, while female part-time typists increased from 6 per cent to 27.6 per cent over the same period

Manufacturing is still a major source of employment for clerks and typists. In 1981, manufacturing (SIC Divisions 2, 3 and 4) employed 17.4 per cent of female clerks (Occupation 6046) and 19.9 per cent of female secretaries (Occupation 6049). The Population Census 1981 (CEN82EA), *Economic Activity, Great Britain*, table 12, pages 233–96, classifies a 10 per cent sample of employment by occupations and by industry. The presumption is that manufacturing has had a proportionate share in the general direct substitution of part-time for full-time clerical and secretarial staff. The indirect substitution is also important. Manufacturing firms, along with others, may change core employment in response to changes in trade, but such fluctuations in business are met largely by the use of temporary, part-time, casual labour and so on. This penumbral labour is often hired indirectly through agencies which are classified to the service sector. In the long term, as manufacturing sub-contracts more and more of its labour requirements to the service sector, the official statistics of manufacturing employment fall more rapidly than the number of people actually working in manufacturing industry.

6   The number of women twenty years and over employed in distribution increased from 890,000 in 1951 to 1,410,000 in 1981, while those in services increased from 2,243,000 to 3,989,000 over the same period (see table 4.3).

7   A summary of the evidence on the low level of manufacturing technology in the United Kingdom is given by Katrak (1982). In particular he measured the increase in the skill-content of British imports compared with its exports 1968–72. A more detailed study by Daly and Jones (1980) on the machine tool industry in Britain, Germany and the United States, shows that British imports of machine tools tended to be of the more advanced type whereas its export of machine tools tended to be of the more standard form which suffered increasing competition in world markets.

8   The odds are that 43,000 extra self-employed jobs will mainly be for those over 25 years. In 1981 there were 160,588 persons in construction employment in the 10 per cent sample of economic activity in Great Britain, and 92 per cent of them were males. Self-employed men formed nearly 24 per cent of male employment in the sample. Within this group only 484 were under twenty years (1 per cent of self-employed males) while the 2,929 young men under 25 years formed 8 per cent. Thus 92 per cent of self-employed males in the construction industry in 1981 were 25 years and over (see Office of Population Census and Surveys (1984) Census 1981 Economic Activity in Great Britain, C EN 81 EA table 13 p. 319).

9   According to *The Times* 12 July 1986, page 3, an unpublished survey by the National Foundation for Educational Research shows that children aged thirteen in England and Wales did worse in arithmetic, algebra and geometry in 1981 than in 1964. This is consistent with the hypothesis of falling standards in the numeracy of pupils. See also Prais (1986b) footnote 16.

10   Which form of production function should be chosen? Popular forms are the Cobb-Douglas, the CES (Constant Elasticity of Substitution) and the

Transcendental Logarithmic (Translog), but there are many others. Should the returns to scale be constant, increasing or decreasing? How should technical progress be introduced? Should it be disembodied applying equally to all inputs? Should it be Harrod-neutral (increasing efficiency of labour), Solow-neutral (increasing efficiency of capital) or Hicks-neutral (increasing efficiency of both labour and capital)? Should technical progress be embodied in particular vintages of capital equipment, or age cohorts of labour? Having chosen an appropriate production function, it is then necessary to derive firms' demands for each of the inputs.

For example, suppose the production function is Cobb-Douglas with disembodied technical progress,

$$y = \alpha \Pi_j x_j^{\beta_j}$$

using the notation of Chapter 3 and with estimates of α for different time periods showing disembodied technical progress through shifts in the production function. Then minimising costs, $\Sigma_j w_j x_j$ subject to this production function, yields the demand for x_j as a log-linear function of relative input prices and output.

A common procedure is to estimate the dual cost function, instead of the primal production function, on the assumption that the competitive equilibrium conditions hold. The translog cost function, used by Abowd *et al.* (1981) and discussed in Chapter 3, is often chosen because it is the dual of a class of production functions which is even larger than the translog production function, as noted by Christensen *et al.* (1975).

Clearly, there are many different ways of estimating the effects of capital equipment on the demand for young labour and there is great scope for controversy.

11 Data for manufacturing are better than for distribution and services. However, note 5 above shows that figures of employment in manufacturing are becoming more misleading as firms sub-contract labour requirements to agencies classified to the service sector. The increasing practice of leasing capital equipment from the finance sector, instead of purchasing it, also affects the figures of capital expenditure in manufacturing which refer to assets owned rather than to assets used. Some correction for this is made possible by the industrial classification of leasing in the notes at the back of the CSO Blue Book (1985) United Kingdom National Income Accounts p. 118.

12 Hamermesh (1985) provides a most helpful discussion of substitutability and the demand for labour. His table 4, pages 74–5, cites six studies which exclude capital, and eight studies which include it but none of the latter refers to the United Kingdom.

13 Asteraki (1984) uses a dynamic translog model to estimate the substitution elasticities in manufacturing and finds that capital and labour are substitutes with positive cross-price elasticities, whether or not restrictions are imposed on the estimation procedure. Helliwell, Sturm, Jarrett and Salou (1985) regard labour and capital as quasi-fixed factors of production with factor utilisation acting as a short-term adjustment variable. However,

using a CES production function approach, they found the elasticity of substitution between labour and capital in the United Kingdom to be positive but less than unity. Holly and Smith (1985) use a translog cost function to estimate the demand equations for labour, capital and energy, and in their table 1 they find that labour and capital are substitutes. They do not impose the Slutsky symmetry conditions, unlike Abowd *et al.* (1981), but they do implicitly assume that time series of factor shares reflect the demand for inputs and they may have the same identification problem. In a later paper, Holly and Smith (1986), the authors impose the symmetry restrictions and find that labour and capital are substitutes.

14   The labour displaced by capital equipment is likely to be young. Many firms reduce their labour by stopping recruitment and allowing natural wastage to reduce employment, thus avoiding trouble with trade unions. A ban on recruitment obviously reduces the job prospects of young people entering the labour market. When redundancies are unavoidable, the principle of 'last in first out' would make it more difficult for young people already in employment to retain their jobs.

15   The Financial Times *Special Report on Work*, 24 July 1986, surveys the substitution of capital equipment for labour in recent years in the article 'The irresistible march of the machine; pp. 6–9.

6   YOUTH UNEMPLOYMENT IN FRANCE AND GERMANY

1   These percentage rates have been read from graphs of time series of unemployment rates for 15–19 year olds in figures 1 and 2 of OECD (1984) *Youth Employment in France*, pages 26–27. Graphs are also given for 20–24 year olds and for 25–54 year olds. No tables of unemployment rates were published although some individual rates are given in the text. Marsden (1986, table 2.1) uses the *Labour Force Sample Survey* to estimate an increase in the unemployment rate of French males aged under twenty from 4.54 per cent in 1973 to 20.7 per cent in 1981, with an alternative estimate for 1981 of 23.2 per cent based on an enlarged ILO concept. For French females under twenty years, his estimated unemployment rates increased from 7.9 per cent in 1973 to 28.6 per cent in 1981, with the ILO alternative estimate of 43.4 per cent.

Unemployment rates for young people in the United Kingdom are published by Wells (1983, table D.17).

2   The German unemployment rates were also read from figures 1 and 2 in OECD (1984). Wagner (1986, table 3.1) shows that the number of unemployed German males under twenty years increased from 56.1 thousand in 1975 to 81.9 thousand in 1984, or by 46 per cent. For young German females under twenty years, unemployment increased from 59.7 thousand in 1975 to 94.9 thousand in 1984, or by 59 per cent.

3   More recent work by Marsden (1986, table 2.2) shows an increase of 2.2 per cent in the number of 15–19 year olds 1968–82, with a 2.6 per cent rise for young males and a 1.9 per cent increase for young females. But even these higher percentage increases cannot account for much of the

upsurge in youth unemployment in France to the very high rates observed for 1982 in table 6.1.

4 For example, the percentage of eighteen year olds (male and female, but excluding apprentices) in full-time education in France increased from 24.4 per cent in 1964/5 to 41.7 per cent in 1982/3.

5 OECD (1983) *Employment Outlook*, table 18, p. 44, shows that in 1981 15.9 per cent of female employment was part-time in France, 25.7 per cent in Germany, and 37.1 per cent in the United Kingdom. Marsden, Trinder and Wagner (1986, *National Institute Economic Review*, no. 117, table 2 p. 44) show that the all ages female activity rates in 1983 were 45.1 per cent for France, 40.1 per cent for Germany, and 44.8 per cent for the United Kingdom. Hence the proportion of females in full-time employment in France is higher than in Germany or the United Kingdom.

6 A useful summary is provided by Ashford (1982, Chapter 6). Further details may be found in Dorion and Guionnet (1983). The absence of a lower earnings limit for social security payments in France is also noted by the Treasury and Civil Service Committee (1983) HC386 p. xxxiv and by the Basic Income Research Group in evidence to House of Lords (1985) p. 157.

7 There is a critical level or ceiling (*plafond*). Since 1967 the employers' contributions to health insurance and so on (*maladie – maternité – invalidité – décès*) have been 8 per cent on the total remuneration, in addition to 5.45 per cent on the remuneration below the ceiling, making a total of 13.45 per cent on the below ceiling wages of those employees who earn more than this limit. This limit was 88,920F per annum from 1 January 1983 (about £17,700). Up to this limit, the employer's total contributions to social security schemes (excluding unemployment) was equivalent to 34.38 per cent of remuneration, compared with the employee's contribution of 10.3 per cent.

7 THE CASE OF RETAIL DISTRIBUTION

1 By June 1986 female part-timers reached 62.3 per cent of all female employees in retail distribution, see table 1.4 (page 512) in the *Employment Gazette*, October 1986.

2 The *first-year* allowance for capital expenditure on plant and machinery (other than motor cars) was 100 per cent before 14 March 1984. It was reduced to 75 per cent 14/3/84 to 30/3/85, to 50 per cent 1/4/85 to 30/3/86, and to zero from 1/4/86. Writing-down allowances of 25 per cent per annum on the reducing balance of the residue of such capital expenditure not covered by first-year allowances may be deducted from profit for purposes of income and corporation tax. Provisions for *initial* allowances for capital expenditure on 'industrial buildings or structure' *exclude* retail shops, showrooms, hotels, offices. Thus in the case of retail distribution the incentives provided by tax allowances relate to the refurbishment rather than the building of shops. But it is new equipment rather than new buildings which are a substitute for labour.

8 SPATIAL ASPECTS OF YOUTH UNEMPLOYMENT

1   The Department of Employment Research Paper by Ashton, Maguire and Garland (1982) argues on page 35 that social security benefits are the same in each town yet youth unemployment is much higher in Sunderland than in St Albans. But this does not mean that social security benefits do not affect youth unemployment. There are many causes of youth unemployment; some are best measured across space, others are best measured over time. Variations in social security benefits are better measured over time, although a case might be made for studying their variation in real terms across different locations. That is, unemployment and social security benefits are worth more in real terms in areas with relatively low living costs, especially costs of accommodation and transport.

2   Garner, Main and Raffe (1987) show that youth unemployment in four Scottish cities is independent of the area in which these youngsters live, apart from the small effect contributed by 'going to a good school'. Personal characteristics of the individuals, and of their families, are the important influences. Richardson (1983) found that specific area effects on youth unemployment in London are not dominant, at least for boys.

3   East Anglia has a much smaller population (under 2 million) than the South-East region (over 17 million) and in terms of numbers the prosperous sector 1 is primarily South-East England.

4   Crampton (1984) qualifies this interpretation of the urban–rural shift of employment. Some rural areas have prospered because of special locational factors (for example, North-East Scotland and oil, East Anglia and container traffic through ports convenient for the European Community) which cannot apply to rural areas in general. Furthermore, some large cities, such as Leeds and Newcastle, have not fared too badly, relative to their regions, partly because of the decentralisation of offices.

5   See note 6 to Chapter 1.

6   The 34 firms above 1,000 employees had about 66 per cent of all employees, if it may be assumed that the size distribution of firms is approximately lognormal.

9 POLICIES FOR YOUTH EMPLOYMENT

1   See Prais and Wagner (1985).

2   The shortcomings of British training and education were noted in Chapters 4 and 5. Chapter 6 summarises the education and training policies of important competitor countries, France and Germany. The concentration of youth unemployment on those without qualifications was noted in Chapter 8.

3   The principle of repeating courses could be adopted without necessarily following the time-period of a year used in France and Germany. Repetition of a term's work (or a half-year's work) might be more acceptable because it reduces the education lag between those who fail and their contemporaries

who pass. On the other hand, assessments each term might be less acceptable than assessments each year.

4   The White Paper, *Working Together – Education and Training*, 1986, *Cmnd*
    9823, announces the Government's intention to expand TVEI from the
    autumn term 1987. Substantial resources will be provided, reaching £84
    million in 1989–90.

5   CSO (1986), *Monthly Digest of Statistics* May, table 3.2, page 18, estimates
    manufacturing employment in June 1985 as 5,533,000 compared with total
    employees in employment of 21,460,000.

6   A possible modification would be to follow the Australian Labour Govern-
    ment and abolish such benefits for the 16–18 year olds after allowing six
    months of benefits to finance job search, as reported in *The Independent*,
    22 June 1987. This 'stick' should be combined with the 'carrot' of an
    improved YTS programme. Such a combination cannot be regarded as
    'conscription'; those who prefer to be employed, self-employed, or work
    in 'the black economy' are still free to do so. Indeed, those who want
    to be self-employed may obtain assistance under the Enterprise Allowance
    Scheme.

7   Full integration, as defined by the Green Paper *Cmnd* 9756 (p. 37) would
    lead to elderly taxpayers and other pensioners paying more, since they
    do not pay national insurance contributions at the moment. This redistribu-
    tion of income might be regarded as undesirable, in which case the scheme
    for integration with limited coverage (paragraph 7.14 p. 39) could be
    adopted. This would exempt the elderly from the combined charges of
    income taxes and national insurance on their earnings, but their investment
    income would be taxed at a separate rate.

8   White (1986) estimates that the cumulative effect of the scheme probably
    reduced unemployment by 200,000.

9   For young people under 25 years, long-term is defined as six months or
    more. For older workers it is a year or more. Table 2.5 shows that in
    1985 some 616.5 thousand young people had unemployment durations of
    six months or more, which is about 39 per cent of 1.58 million.

10 Of course, such ideas are not new; the use of public works to reduce unem-
    ployment has a long history and the paradox of having extensive slums
    and mass unemployment of building workers entered the deliberations of
    the Macmillan Committee in 1930 (see Committee on Finance and Industry
    (1931)). This committee was chaired by H. P. Macmillan, K.C., later Lord
    Macmillan, Lord of Appeal in Ordinary 1930–39. See Addendum I (by
    Thos. Allen, E. Bevin, J. M. Keynes, R. McKenna, J. Frater Taylor and
    A. A. G. Tulloch), page 207, paragraph 51(i):
    '(i) A considerable part of the larger towns and industrial centres of
    the country need rebuilding and replanning on a comprehensive scale.
    At present they offer neither beauty nor convenience nor health. Much
    of the industrial housing of the country is of an age when buildings
    of that character are, of necessity, only fit to be demolished. It seems
    an insanity to keep a large proportion of the building trade out of employ-
    ment when this is the case.'

The objections to such policies have an equally long history; increases in Government expenditure have to be financed, and increased taxation or borrowing might crowd out other investment expenditure so that there would be little increase in total investment and little increase in total employment. In the 1930s this crowding-out hypothesis was called 'the Treasury view', although the debate between Keynes and Sir Richard Hopkins showed that the Treasury view did not rely solely on neo-classical interest rate theory but was also based on the likely effects of such public expenditure on business confidence. See Committee on Finance and Industry (1931) Minutes of Evidence 22 May 1930 reprinted in J. M. Keynes (1981). Sir Richard Hopkins argued that although a public works scheme might reduce unemployment in a particular place in the short run, it might lead to more unemployment in the longer run if the scheme were regarded as unsound by the public. An extreme example of an unsound scheme would be to break all the windows in London and use unemployed people to repair them. If business confidence were lowered, capital would flow abroad. Other objections to massive public works schemes such as new road systems were that they might lead to increased prices for construction materials, and to increased profits for some industries (quarries) which were already prosperous. In addition, it would take years to deal with all the objections to new roads from landowners, conservation groups and the like so that such schemes would not begin to reduce unemployment for some time. In any case, when the new road system was completed it would not necessarily revive British exports which were suffering from intensive international competition.

11 Committee on Finance and Industry (1931), Addendum III by Professor T. E. Gregory, page 229., paragraph 14:

Gregory: 'So long as capital equipment and labour-power are out of employment, and current savings are hoarded because of lack of confidence, it is, of course, true that national works are not impossible because they cannot be financed except at the expense of withdrawing resources from other possible avenues of employment. But the most urgent problem which we have to face concerns the export industries, and it is not easy to see how plans of national development would much assist these industries in the short run. Development works of any kind will: (i) absorb unemployed labour of *some* kind; (ii) give assistance to the constructional trades ...; (iii) indirectly stimulate demand for other labour through increasing the purchasing power of workers and employers engaged in the constructional trades. ... But the indirect demand under heading (iii) will not necessarily be confined to home products, so that, to the extent that imports of foodstuffs and raw materials increase, no direct stimulus to home demand will result under this head.'

12 It is worth quoting their views from Howson and Winch (1977):

'It may be that in particular cases the difficulties could be overcome and a workable scheme could be devised in which the disadvantages were at a minimum and the advantages to employment at a maximum. If and where this is so it appears to the majority of us (Mr Keynes,

Professor Pigou and Sir Josiah Stamp) that the cases for wage subsidies in respect of *additional* employees at a rate less than the present rate of unemployment pay is a strong one. We have not investigated any particular proposals under this head. One of us however (Mr Henderson), is of opinion that it would be impossible to frame any scheme of subsidies which would not by its repercussions do more harm than good, and holds strongly that the path of subsidies to wages is one which should be avoided. If attempted in particular industries, subsidies would need to be so framed that their temporary character was emphasised; and provision would need to be made for their gradual abolition in such a way as not to create disturbance. Subsidies to wages in particular industries, as a permanent system, are, in our view, highly undesirable. Moreover, it must be remembered that any system of subsidies, whether general or particular, is difficult to administer without risk of abuse.'

13 Compare the Committee on Finance and Industry (1931), Addendum 1 page 205:

(ii) 'It is feared that State-aided schemes are likely to put some burden on the Budget and therefore to lead to the evils of increased taxation. If, however, we lump together – as we should for the purposes of this argument – the Budget and the Unemployment Fund, we feel quite confident that the relief to the Unemployment Fund and the additional yield of taxation, resulting from the increased employment provided by the schemes in question, would materially outweigh the direct cost of the schemes to the State.'

APPENDIX 3   TRENDS IN UNEMPLOYMENT

1 This claim is strongly supported by his Figure 4.5 (page 148), but receives weak support from his Figure 4.7 (page 150) which compares earnings of young men with those of men aged 40–49.

2 This amounts to arguing that increasing aggregate demand is not *sufficient* by itself to remove mass unemployment. But it might still be a *necessary* condition for the removal of mass unemployment, though insufficient without the introduction of some form of incomes policy. However, the Government rejects an incomes policy and prefers to leave employers and employees free to negotiate pay (*Cmnd* 8745 (1982) para. 16, p. 17).

REFERENCES

Abowd, J., Layard, R. and Nickell, S. (1981), The demand for labour by age and sex, London School of Economics, Centre for Labour Studies, Working paper no. 110.

Armstrong, H. and Taylor, J. (1987), *Regional Policy: the Way Forward*, London, Employment Institute.

Artis, M., Bladen-Hovell, R., Karakitsos, E. and Dwolatzky, B. (1984), 'The effects of economic policy: 1979–82', *National Institute Economic Review*, no. 108, pp. 54–67.

Ashford, D. E. (1982), *Policy and Politics in France: Living with Uncertainty*, Philadelphia, Temple University Press.

Ashton, D. N. and Maguire, M. J. (1986), Young adults in the labour market, Department of Employment research paper no. 55.

Ashton, D. N., Maguire, M. J. and Garland, V. (1982), Youth in the labour market, Department of Employment research paper no. 34.

Ashworth, J. (1982), The supply of labour, in Creedy, J. and Thomas, B. (Eds), *The Economics of Labour*, London, Butterworths.

Asteraki, D. J. (1984), A dynamic 'translog' model of substitution technologies in UK manufacturing industry, Bank of England discussion paper no. 7.

Atkinson, J. and Meager, N. (1986), *Changing Working Patterns*, London, National Economic Development Office.

Barnett, C. (1986), *The Audit of War*, London, Macmillan.

Begg, I., Moore, B. and Rhodes, J. (1986), Chapter 2 in Hausner, V. A. (Ed.), *Critical Issues in Urban Economic Development*, vol. I, Oxford, Clarendon Press.

Brittan, S. (1975), *Second Thoughts on Full Employment Policy*, London, Barry Rose for Centre for Policy Studies.

Britton, A. (1986), *The Trade Cycle in Britain 1958–1982*, Cambridge, Cambridge University Press.

Britton, A. (1986a), 'Employment policy in the public sector' in Hart, P. E. (Ed.) (1986). *op. cit.*

Brodie, I. (1985), *Distributive Trades*, SPRU Institute of Manpower Studies, University of Sussex, London, Gower Press.

Brown, C. V. (1980), *Taxation and Incentives to Work*, Oxford University Press.

Buck, N. and Gordon, I. (1986), The beneficiaries of employment growth: an analysis of the experience of disadvantaged groups in expanding labour markets, in Hausner, V. A. (Ed.) *Critical Issues in Urban Economic Development*, vol. II, Oxford University Press.

Cannan, E. (1930), 'The problem of unemployment; a review of the 'Post-war Unemployment Problem' by Henry Clay', *Economic Journal*, *40*, pp. 45–55.

Casson, M. (1983), *Economics of Unemployment*, Oxford, Martin Robertson.

Chancellor of the Exchequer (1980), *The taxation of husband and wife*, Cmnd 8093, London, HMSO.

Chancellor of the Exchequer (1986), *The reform of personal taxation, Cmnd* 9756, London, HMSO.

Cheshire, P. C. (1973), *Regional Unemployment Differences in Great Britain,* Cambridge University Press.

Cheshire, P. C. (1979), 'Inner areas as spatial labour markets: a critique of the Inner Area Studies, *Urban Studies, 16,* pp. 29–43.

Christensen, L. R., Jorgenson, D. W. and Lau, L. J. (1975), 'Transcendental logarithmic utility functions', *American Economic Review, 65,* no. 3, pp. 367–82.

Clay, H. (1929), *The Post-war Unemployment Problem,* London, Macmillan.

Clifton, R. and Tatton-Brown, C. (1979), Impact of employment legislation on small firms, Department of Employment research paper no. 6.

Committee on Finance and Industry (1931), Report of the Committee appointed by HM Treasury, June 1931, *Cmd.* 3897, London, HMSO.

Confederation of British Industries (1985), Cutting unemployment now: the opportunity for the 1986 budget, November.

Craig, C. and Wilkinson, F. (1985), Pay and employment in four retail trades, Department of Employment research paper no. 51.

Crampton, G. (1984), Urban–rural shift in Britain: some new evidence from 1971–81 male unemployment rate changes, University of Reading Discussion Papers in Economics, Series C, no. 21.

Daly, A. and Jones, D. T. (1980), 'The machine tool industry in Britain, Germany and the United States', *National Institute Economic Review,* no. 92, May, pp. 53–63.

Daly, A., Hitchens, D. M. W. and Wagner, K. (1985), 'Productivity, machinery and skills in a sample of British and German manufacturing plants', *National Institute Economic Review,* no. 111, February, pp. 48–61.

Daniel, W. W. and Stilgoe, E. (1978), The impact of employment protection laws, Policy Studies Institute, XLIV, no. 577.

Davis, N. (1986), 'Training for change' in Hart, P. E. (Ed.) *Unemployment and Labour Market Policies,* Aldershot, Gower Publishing Co.

Deaton, A, and Muellbauer, J. (1980), *Economics and Consumer Behavior,* Cambridge University Press.

Department of Employment (1985), *Lifting the burden, Cmnd* 9571, London, HMSO.

Department of Employment (1986), *Building Businesses ... not Barriers, Cmnd* 9794, London, HMSO.

Doeringer, P. B. and Piore, M. J. (1971), *Internal Labor Markets and Manpower Analysis,* Lexington, Mass, Heath Lexington.

Dorion, G. and Guionnet, A. (1983), *La Sécurité Sociale,* in Que sais-je? series, Paris, Presses Universitaires de France.

Economists Report to the Economic Advisory Council, *see* Howson and Winch (1977).

Ermisch, J. (1983), *The Political Economy of Demographic Change,* London, Heinemann.

Evans, S., Goodman, J. and Hargreaves, L. (1985), Unfair dismissal law and employment practice, Department of Employment Research Paper no. 53.

Fisher, G. (1980), Propositions, principles and methods: the linear hypothesis and structural change, Queen's University, Kingston, Ontario, Department of Economics Discussion Paper no. 410.

Garner, C. L., Main, B. G. M. and Raffe, D. (1981), 'Local variations in school-leaver unemployment within a large city', *British Journal of Education and Work, 1*.

Gomulka J. and Stern, N. (1986), The employment of married women in the UK: 1970–1983, London School of Economics, Discussion paper no. 98, ESRC Programme on Taxation, Incentives and the Distribution of Income.

Gordon, I. (1985), Unemployment in London, Urban and Regional Studies Unit, University of Kent Discussion Paper.

Green, A. E., Owen, D. W., Champion, A. G., Goddard, J. B. and Coombes, M. G. (1985), What contribution can labour migration make to reducing unemployment? Centre for Urban and Regional Studies, University of Newcastle upon Tyne.

Hall, S. G., Henry, S. G. B., Markandya, A. and Pemberton, M. (1985), A disequilibrium model of the UK labour market: some estimates using rational expectations, National Institute of Economic and Social Research Discussion Paper no. 102.

Hamermesh, D. S. (1985), Substitution between different categories of labour, relative wages and youth unemployment, OECD Economic Studies, no. 5, Autumn, pp. 57–85.

Harris, J. R. and Todaro, M. P. (1970), 'Migration, unemployment and development: a two sector analysis', *American Economic Review, 60*, pp. 126–42.

Hart, P. E. (Ed.) (1986), *Unemployment and Labour Market Policies*, Aldershot, Gower Publishing Co.

Hart, P. E. (1986a), 'Youth unemployment and relative wages in the UK: a survey of the evidence', *Economic Perspectives, 4*, pp. 283–314.

Hart, P. E. and Trinder, C. (1986), 'Employment protection, national insurance, income tax and youth unemployment in the UK' in Hart, P. E. (Ed.) (1986), *op. cit.*

Harvey, A. C. (1976), 'An alternative proof and generalisation of a test for structural change', *American Statistician, 30*, pp. 122–3.

Harvey, A. C. (1981), *Time Series Models*, Oxford, Philip Allan.

Hayek, F. A. (1967), *Studies in Philosophy, Politics and Economics*, London, Routledge and Kegan Paul.

Helliwell, J., Sturm, P., Jarrett, P. and Salou, G. (1985), Aggregate supply in interlink: model specification and empirical results, OECD Department of Economics and Statistics, Working Paper no. 26.

Holly, S. and Smith, P. (1985), Production, inventories and prices: the supply side in the LBS model, London Business School Discussion Paper no. 150.

Holly, S. and Smith, P. (1986), Inter-related factor demands for manufacturing: a dynamic translog cost function approach, Centre for Economic Forecasting London Business School, Discussion Paper no. 18–86.

House of Commons (1983), Third special report of the Treasury and Civil Service Commitee, *HC* 386, London, HMSO.

House of Lords (1982), Report from the Select Committee of the House of

Lords on Unemployment, (142) vol. III, *Minutes of Evidence*, Lord Roberthall's evidence, pp. 627–8, London, HMSO.

House of Lords (1982a), *Voluntary part-time work*. Select Committee on the European Communities, *HL* 216, London, HMSO.

House of Lords (1985), *Income Taxation and Equal Treatment for Men and Women*, Select Committee on the European Communities (*HL* 15).

Howson, S. and Winch, D. (1977), *The Economic Advisory Council 1930–39: A Study in Economic Advice during Depression and Recovery*, Cambridge University Press.

Hughes, P. (1982), 'Flows on and off the unemployment register', *Employment Gazette, 90*, December, pp. 527–30.

Hutchinson, G., Barr, N. and Drobny, A. (1979), A sequential approach to the dynamic specification of the demand for young male labour in Great Britain, Queen Mary College, London, Department of Economics Working Paper no. 60.

Hutchinson, G., Barr, N. A. and Drobny, A. (1984), 'The employment of young males in a segmented labour market: the case of Great Britain', *Applied Economics, 16*, pp. 187–204.

Incomes Data Services (1986), *Private Sector Part-timers*, IDS Study 374, London, Incomes Data Services Ltd.

Jackman, R. and Roper, S. (1985), Structural unemployment, Centre for Labour Economics, London School of Economics, Discussion paper no. 233.

Jones, I. S. (1985), Pay relativities and the provision of workplace-based training, National Institute of Economic and Social Research Discussion Paper no. 77.

Jones, I. S. (1986), 'Trainee pay and costs of vocational training in Britain and Germany', Chapter 10 in Marsden, D. (Ed.), *Youth Pay and Employers' Recruitment Practice for Young Workers in EEC Countries*, London School of Economics and Political Science.

Junankar, P. N. and Neale, A. J. (1985), Relative wages and the youth labour market, Institute for Employment Research (University of Warwick), Discussion Paper no. 29.

Kane, P. (1986), 'Young people's pay and employment', Chapter 11 in Commission of the European Communities, *Social Europe*, Supplement on youth pay and employers' recruitment practices for young people in the Community, CE-ND-85-009, EN-C, Luxembourg, EC, pp. 129–34.

Katrak, H. (1982), 'Labour skills, R and D and capital requirements in the international trade and investment of the United Kingdom 1968–78', *National Institute Economic Review*, no. 101, August, pp. 38–47.

Keynes, J. M. (1981), *The Collected Writings of John Maynard Keynes*, vol. XX, *Activities 1929–31: Rethinking Employment and Unemployment Policies*, London, Macmillan; Cambridge University Press.

Layard, R., Metcalf, D. and O'Brien, R. (1986), 'A new deal for the long-term unemployed', in Hart, P. E. (Ed.) (1986), *op. cit.*

Lecraw, D. (1985), 'Singapore', Chapter 12 in Dunning, J. H. (Ed.), *Multinational Enterprises, Economic Structure and International Competitiveness*, Chichester, John Wiley.

Lewis, J. A. and Armstrong, K. M. (1986), 'Skill shortages and recruitment problems in West Midlands engineering industry', *National Westminster Bank Review*, November, pp. 45–56.

Liepmann, K. (1960), *Apprenticeship: an Enquiry into its Adequacy under Modern Conditions*, London, Routledge & Kegan Paul.

Lindbeck, A. and Snower, D. J. (1985), 'Explanations of unemployment', *Oxford Review of Economic Policy*, *1*, no. 2, pp. 34–59.

Lobban, P. (1986), Comment on 'A new deal for the long-term unemployed' by Layard, R., Metcalf, D. and O'Brien, R. *op. cit.*

Lynch, L. M. (1983), 'Job search and youth unemployment', *Oxford Economic Papers*, November supplement, *35*, pp. 596–606.

Lynch, L. M. (1985), 'State dependency in youth unemployment: a lost generation?' *Journal of Econometrics*, *28*, pp. 71–84.

Lynch, L. M. (1987), 'Individual differences in the youth labour market: a cross section analysis of London youth', Chapter 9 in Junankar, P. N. (Ed.), *From School to Unemployment?* Basingstoke, Macmillan.

Lynch, L. and Richardson, R. (1982), 'Unemployment of young workers in Britain', *British Journal of Industrial Relations*, *XX*, pp. 362–71.

Maddala, G. S. and Nelson, F. D. (1974), 'Maximum likelihood methods for models of markets in disequilibrium', *Econometrica*, *42*, pp. 1013–30.

Main, B. G. M. and Raffe, D. (1983), 'Determinants of employment and unemployment among school leavers', *Scottish Journal of Political Economy*, *30*, pp. 1–17.

Makeham, P. (1980), Youth unemployment, Department of Employment Research Paper no. 10.

Manley, P. and Sawbridge, D. (1980), 'Women at work', *Lloyds Bank Review*, no. 135, January.

Manpower Services Commission (1978), *Young people and work*, Manpower Studies no. 19781, London, HMSO.

Marsden, D. (1985), 'Youth pay in Britain compared with France, and FR Germany since 1966', *British Journal of Industrial Relations*, *23*, pp. 399–414.

Marsden, D. (1986), 'Youth employment in France', Chapter 2 in Hart, P. E. *et al.*, Structure of Youth Employment, NIESR Report to EEC.

Marsden, D. and Ryan, P. (1986), 'Where do young workers work? Youth employment by industry in various European economies', *British Journal of Industrial Relations*, *24*, pp. 83–102.

Marsden, D., Trinder, C. and Wagner, K. (1986), 'Measures to reduce youth unemployment in Britain, France and West Germany', *National Institute Economic Review*, no. 117, pp. 43–51.

Martin, J. P. (1983), 'Effects of the minimum wage on the youth labour market in North America and France', *OECD Economic Outlook*, Occasional studies, Paris, OECD.

Martin, J. and Roberts, C. (1984), *Women and Employment: a Lifetime Perspective*, Department of Employment and Office of Population Censuses and Surveys, London, HMSO.

Matthews, R., Feinstein, C. and Odling-Smee, J. (1982), *British Economic Growth 1856–1973*, Oxford, Clarendon Press.

Merrilees, W. J. and Wilson, R. A. (1979), Disequilibrium in the labour market for young people in Great Britain, University of Warwick Manpower Research Group, Discussion Paper no. 10.

Micklewright, J. (1986), 'Unemployment and incentives to work: policy and evidence in the 1980s', in Hart, P. E. (Ed.) (1986), *op. cit.*

Morris, D, and Sinclair, P. (1985), 'The unemployment problem in the 1980s', *Oxford Review of Economic Policy, 1*, no. 2, pp. 1–19.

Narendranathan, W., Nickell, S. and Stern, J. (1985), 'Unemployment benefits revisited', *Economic Journal, 95*, pp. 307–29.

National Economic Development Office (1985), *Employment Perspectives and the Distributive Trades*, London, NEDO.

National Economic Development Office (1986), *Changing Working Patterns*, a report by J. Atkinson and N. Meager, London, NEDO.

National Economic Development Office (1986), *Young People's Employment in Retailing*, a report by C. Trinder, London, NEDO.

National Institute of Economic and Social Research (1983), *National Institute Economic Review*, no. 106, Chapter III, pp. 39–48.

Nelson, C. R. and Kang, H. (1984), 'Pitfalls in the use of time as an explanatory variable in regression', *Journal of Business and Economic Statistics, 2*, pp. 73–82.

Nelson, C. R. and Plosser, C. I. (1982), 'Trends and random walks in macroeconomic time-series: some evidence and implications', *Journal of Monetary Economics, 10*, pp. 139–62.

Neubourg, C. de (1985), 'Part-time work: an international quantitative comparison', *International Labour Review, 124*, pp. 559–76.

Nickell, S. (1982), 'The determinants of equilibrium unemployment in Britain', *Economic Journal, 92*, pp. 555–75.

OECD (1980), *Youth Unemployment: the Causes and Consequences*, Paris, OECD.

OECD (1984), *Youth Employment in France: Recent Strategies*, Paris, OECD.

OECD (1985) (1986), *Employment Outlook*, September issues, Paris, OECD.

Olson, M. (1982), *The Rise and Decline of Nations*, New Haven, Yale University Press.

Peden, G. C. (1979), *British Rearmament and the Treasury: 1932–39*, Edinburgh, Scottish Academic Press.

Pemberton, J. (1981), A two-sector model of inflation, unemployment and aggregate demand, University of Reading Discussion Paper in Economics, Series A, no. 123.

Pemberton, J. (1984), 'Equilibrium unemployment and the long-run Phillips curve in a partially unionised economy', *Manchester School, LII*, no. 4, pp. 402–16.

Phelps Brown, E. H. (1959), *The Growth of British Industrial Relations*, London, Macmillan.

Phelps Brown, E. H. and Hopkins, J. V. (1950), 'The course of wage-rates in five countries, 1860–1939', *Oxford Economic Papers, 2*, pp. 226–96.

Pigou, A. C. (1927), 'Wage policy and unemployment', *Economic Journal, 37*, pp. 355–68.

Pissarides, C. (1986), 'Unemployment and vacancies in Britain', *Economic Policy*, 2, pp. 499–559.

Pool, A. G. (1938), *Wage Policy in Relation to Industrial Fluctuations*, London, Macmillan.

Prais, S. J. (1981), 'Vocational qualifications of the labour force in Britain and Germany', *National Institute Economic Review*, no. 98, November.

Prais, S. J. (1986a), Comment on Davis, N. 'Training for Change' in Hart, P. E. (Ed.) (1986), *op. cit.*

Prais, S. J. (1986b), Educating for productivity: comparisons of Japanese and English schooling and vocational preparation, National Institute of Economic and Social Research Discussion Paper no. 121.

Prais, S. J. (1987), Productivity and management: the training of foremen in Britain and Germany, National Institute of Economic and Social Research Discussion Paper (forthcoming).

Prais, S. J. and Steedman, H. (1986), 'Vocational training in France and Britain: the building trades', *National Institute Economic Review*, no. 116, pp. 45–55.

Prais, S. J. and Wagner, K. (1983), 'Some practical aspects of human capital investment: training standards in five occupations in Britain and Germany', *National Institute Economic Review*, no. 105, August.

Prais, S. J. and Wagner, K. (1985), 'Schooling standards in England and Germany: some comparisons bearing on economic performance', *National Institute Economic Review*, no. 112, pp. 53–76.

Rajan, A. (1985), *Job Subsidies: Do They Work*, Institute of Manpower Studies Series, Aldershot, Gower Publishing Co.

Rajan, A. and Pearson, R. (1986). *UK Occupation and Employment Trends to 1990*, London, Butterworths.

Rice, P. G. (1986), 'Juvenile unemployment, relative wages and social security in Great Britain', *Economic Journal*, 96, pp. 352–74.

Richardson, R. (1983), *Unemployment and the Inner City: a Study of School Leavers in London*, Department of the Environment: Inner Cities Research Programme 10.

Roberthall (1982), Lord Roberthall's evidence to Select Committee of the House of Lords on Unemployment, Vol. III, *Minutes of Evidence*, pp. 627–8 (142-III).

Roberts, K., Dench, S. and Richardson, D. (1986), 'Youth labour markets in the 1980s', *Department of Employment Gazette*, July, 94, pp. 241–6.

Robinson, O. and Wallace, J. (1974), 'Part-time employment and low pay in retail distribution in Britain', *Industrial Relations Journal*, 5, pp. 38–56.

Robinson, O. and Wallace, J. (1978), Evidence to the Royal Commission on the Distribution of Income and Wealth Report no. 6, *Lower Incomes*, pp. 460–77.

Robinson, O. and Wallace, J. (1984), Part-time employment and sex discrimination legislation in Great Britain, Department of Employment Research Paper no. 43.

Roy, A. D. and Wenban-Smith, G. (1983), Trends in UK productivity: a production function approach, National Institute of Economic and Social Research Discussion Paper no. 59.

Saville, I. D. and Gardiner, K. L. (1986), 'Stagflation in the UK since 1970: a model-based explanation', *National Institute Economic Review*, no. 117, pp. 52–69.

Schoer, K. (1986), 'Teilzeitbeschäftigung in Grossbritannien und der Bundesrepublik Deutschland', *WSI-Mitteilungen*, 1/1986, pp. 21–9.

Standing, G. (1983), 'The notion of structural unemployment', *International Labour Review, 122*, no. 2, pp. 137–53.

Symons, E. and Walker, I. (1986), Transferable allowances: some questions answered, University of Manchester, Department of Economics, mimeo.

Thatcher, A. R. (1976), 'Statistics of unemployment in the United Kingdom' in Worswick, G. D. N. (Ed.) *The Concept and Measurement of Involuntary Unemployment*, Boulder, Colorado, Westview Press.

Trinder, C. (1985), Youth unemployment: a case study: young women in distribution, National Institute of Economic and Social Research, mimeo.

Trinder, C. (1986), *Young People's Employment in Retailing*, National Institute of Economic and Social Research Report for NEDO Distributive Trades Development Committee.

Unemployment Bulletin (1986), Seventeen statistical sleights, Issue 20, Summer 1986, pp. 14–15, London, Unemployment Unit.

University of Warwick, Institute of Employment Research (1985), Review of the Economy and Employment, 1985, volume 1.

Wagner, K. (1986), 'Youth employment in Germany', Chapter 3 in Hart, P. E. *et al. Structure of Youth Employment*, NIESR Report to EEC.

Wells, W. (1983), The relative pay and employment of young people, Department of Employment Research Paper no. 42.

White, M. (1986), 'Working time and employment: a negotiable issue? Chapter 2 in Hart, P. E. (Ed.) (1986), *op. cit.*

Williams, G. (1957), *Recruitment to the Skilled Trades*, London, Routledge and Kegan Paul.

Willke, G. (1982), 'The structuralist diagnosis and policy menu' in Maddison, A. and Wilpstra, B. S. (Eds), *Unemployment: the European Perspective*, London, Croom Helm.

INDEX

THE NATIONAL INSTITUTE OF ECONOMIC
AND SOCIAL RESEARCH
PUBLICATIONS IN PRINT

published by
THE CAMBRIDGE UNIVERSITY PRESS
(available from booksellers, or in case of difficulty from the publishers)

THE NATIONAL INSTITUTE OF ECONOMIC AND SOCIAL RESEARCH

publishes regularly

THE NATIONAL INSTITUTE ECONOMIC REVIEW

A quarterly analysis of the general economic situation in the United Kingdom and overseas, with forecasts eighteen months ahead. The last issue each year usually contains an assessment of medium-term prospects. There are also in most issues special articles on subjects of interest to academic and business economists.

Annual subscriptions, £45.00 (home), and £60.00 (abroad), also single issues for the current year, £12.50 (home) and £18.00 (abroad), are available from NIESR, 2 Dean Trench Street, Smith Square, London, SW1P 3HE.

Subscriptions at the special reduced price of £18.00 p.a. are available to students in the United Kingdom and Irish Republic on application to the Secretary of the Institute.

Back numbers and reprints of issues which have gone out of stock are distributed by Wm. Dawson and Sons Ltd., Cannon House, Park Farm Road, Folkestone. Microfiche copies for the years 1959–84 are available from E P Microform Ltd., Bradford Road, East Ardsley, Wakefield, Yorks.

Published by

HEINEMANN EDUCATIONAL BOOKS
(distributed by Gower Publishing Company and available from booksellers).

DEMAND MANAGEMENT
Edited by MICHAEL POSNER. 1978. pp. 256. £6.50 net.

DE-INDUSTRIALISATION
Edited by FRANK BLACKABY. 1979. pp. 282. £12.95 (paperback) net.

BRITAIN IN EUROPE
Edited by WILLIAM WALLACE. 1980. pp. 224. £8.50 (paperback) net.

THE FUTURE OF PAY BARGAINING
Edited by FRANK BLACKABY. 1980. pp. 256. £16.00 (hardback), £7.50 (paperback) net.

INDUSTRIAL POLICY AND INNOVATION
Edited by CHARLES CARTER. 1981. pp. 250. £18.50 (hardback), £7.50 (paperback) net.

THE CONSTITUTION OF NORTHERN IRELAND
Edited by DAVID WATT. 1981. pp. 233. £19.50 (hardback), £9.50 (paperback) net.

RETIREMENT POLICY. THE NEXT FIFTY YEARS
Edited by MICHAEL FOGARTY. 1982. pp. 224. £17.50 (hardback), £7.50 (paperback) net.

SLOWER GROWTH IN THE WESTERN WORLD
Edited by R.C.O. MATTHEWS. 1982. pp. 182. £19.50 (hardback), £9.50 (paperback) net.

NATIONAL INTERESTS AND LOCAL GOVERNMENT
Edited by KEN YOUNG. 1983. pp. 180. £17.50 (hardback), £9.50 (paperback) net.

EMPLOYMENT OUTPUT AND INFLATION
Edited by A.J.C. BRITTON. 1983. pp. 208. £25.00 net.

THE TROUBLED ALLIANCE. ATLANTIC RELATIONS IN THE 1980s
Edited by LAWRENCE FREEDMAN. 1983. pp. 176. £19.50 (hardback), £7.50 (paperback) net.

EDUCATION AND ECONOMIC PERFORMANCE
Edited by G.D.N. WORSWICK. 1984. pp. 152. £18.50 net.

Published by
GOWER PUBLISHING COMPANY LTD

ENERGY SELF-SUFFICIENCY FOR THE UK
Edited by ROBERT BELGRAVE and MARGARET CORNELL. 1985. pp. 224. £19.50 net.

THE FUTURE OF BRITISH DEFENCE POLICY
Edited by JOHN ROPER. 1985. pp. 214. £18.50 net.

ENERGY MANAGEMENT: CAN WE LEARN FROM OTHERS?
By GEORGE F. RAY. 1985. pp. 131. £19.50 net.

UNEMPLOYMENT AND LABOUR MARKET POLICIES
Edited by P.E. HART. 1986. pp. 230. £19.50 net.

NEW PRIORITIES IN PUBLIC SPENDING
Edited by M.S. LEVITT. 1987. PP. 136. £17.50 NET.